"CHURCH CONTROL OR **BIRTH CONTROL**":

Margaret Sanger's Propaganda Campaign against the Catholic Church

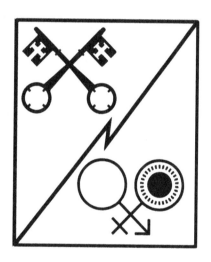

By Nicholas Kaminsky, M.A.

MANKATO, MINNESOTA
INTO YOUR HANDS LLC
2015

Into Your Hands LLC
Mankato, Minnesota
www.intoyourhandsllc.com

ISBN 10: 0985754338

ISBN-13: 978-0-9857543-3-4

Library of Congress Subject Headings

Birth Control–United States–History

Sanger, Margaret, 1879–1966

Catholic Church–United States–History

Freedom of Religion

First Printing, August 2015

CONTENTS

For my parents

PREFACE

This little book started in 2010 as my master's thesis. Since then, it has undergone significant and much-needed revision in order to make it into what I hope will be a readable and informative work. While discerning readers may recognize my partiality for the Church, I have sought to be fair toward Sanger and have attempted to present her propaganda campaign in a scholarly way by letting her own words speak for her, within their proper context.

I believe the work I present here is genuinely significant for modern-day audiences, especially in light of the ongoing conflict over the controversial Patient Protection and Affordable Care Act, more commonly known as Obamacare. This hotly debated 2010 law contains a mandate requiring that employer-provided health insurance plans cover contraceptive services. Numerous organizations, both Catholic and non-Catholic, have filed lawsuits against the government, arguing that this mandate is a violation of their right to religious freedom. As of June 30, 2015, the U.S. Supreme Court has granted relief to some of these conscientious employers, but the fight over the policy continues on numerous other fields, not the least of which is the battleground of public opinion.

The final result of the Obamacare conflict remains to be seen, but those who read this book will understand, if I have written it well, just how dramatically the tables have turned against religious supporters of natural procreation over the course of the last century. We have come a long way since the days when government officials arrested Sanger for violating anti-obscenity statutes. She would undoubtedly be pleased to see the state now backing her position through the force of law, and she would derive no small level of satisfaction from witnessing the uncomfortable situation in which her "arch-enemy," the Catholic Church, now finds itself.

Nicholas Kaminsky

INTRODUCTION

"The Vatican on Tuesday clarified the remarks of Pope Benedict XVI. Again." Following this clever introduction, Jason Horowitz of *The Washington Post* explained in December 2010 how Vatican officials were scrambling to make clear that the pope had not, despite popular opinion to the contrary, condoned the use of condoms in an interview he gave for a new book, *Light of the World: The Pope, the Church and the Signs of the Times.* Horowitz continued, "The Vatican said Benedict's comments about condom use had been 'repeatedly manipulated for ends and interests which are entirely foreign.'"[1]

With these words Horowitz more or less wrapped up the extensive media coverage of what many had believed was a papal compromise regarding the Catholic Church's strict condemnation of artificial means of birth control.[2] This was not the first time the pope had found himself in a controversial position on the topic. During a May 2009 visit to Africa, he stated that condoms were not the answer to the AIDS problem,

---

[1]Jason Horowitz, "In Rome, Clarifying the Pope's Statements on Big Issues Has Become a Full-time Job," *The Washington Post*, December 21, 2010. http://www.washingtonpost.com/wp-dyn/content/article/2010/12/21/AR2010122106109.htm (accessed February 5, 2010).

[2]The expression "artificial means of birth control" commonly refers to any means of limiting conception other than complete or periodic abstinence from sex.

and that their use could even exacerbate the situation. He received strong criticism for these comments from a wide range of people, including Rebecca Hodes of the Treatment Action Campaign. Echoing a sentiment apparently felt by many others, Hodes said of Benedict, "His opposition to condoms conveys that religious dogma is more important to him than the lives of Africans."[3]

The media frenzy surrounding the pope's remarks, especially the statement by Hodes, conveys an important message. In popular belief, the Catholic Church is the sole major opponent of birth control and is so because of its insistence on clinging to an out-of-date and non-pragmatic absolute moral code. Many wonder how the Church can maintain its intransigence in the face of widespread human suffering. They attribute the Church's position to lack of scientific understanding or to a desire to maintain power through moral control. It is likely such commentators do not realize the extent to which their views of the Catholic position on birth control have been shaped by the propaganda of early birth control advocates.

In the United States, the name of Margaret Sanger is nearly synonymous with the birth control movement. In fact, she coined the term. As the founder of the predecessor to Planned Parenthood Federation of America and the first head of International Planned Parenthood, she was the best-known crusader for the legalization of birth control in the country. She was also a skillful propagandist and was fiercely anti-Catholic.[4] Moreover, as this book will demonstrate, Sanger saw her birth control crusade as a moral revolution against the unchanging structure of morality most clearly represented by the Catholic Church. In order to carry out this revolution, she

---

3"Pope: Condoms Not the Answer in AIDS Fight," Africa on msnbc.com. http://www.msnbc.msn.com/id/29734328/ns/world_news-africa/ (accessed February 5, 2010).

4This first predecessor to Planned Parenthood was the American Birth Control League, founded in 1921.

waged a propaganda campaign against the Church in which she portrayed it not only as the sole enemy of birth control, but by extension as the enemy of liberty and science. By linking her birth control revolution with the tradition of the American Revolution through the use of patriotic and anti-Catholic rhetoric, she depicted her fight for birth control as a struggle for American freedom against the tyranny of the Catholic Church.

Sanger's animosity toward the Church sprang from as far back as her early childhood, especially from her radical father's conflicts with Church leaders and his disdain for Catholic doctrine. Toward the end of her career, Sanger appeared on *The Mike Wallace Interview,* during which time Wallace asked her if perhaps she was driven by her anti-Catholic background to campaign for birth control as "a way to fight the Church."[5] Sanger strongly denied it, but even if anti-Catholicism was not the founding principle of her birth control crusade, it certainly played a major role in her campaigns. While her biographers readily explain her conflict with the Church over birth control, they do not fully show the way she used that conflict to exploit American anti-Catholicism in order to further her goals.[6]

One scholar who has demonstrated the way Sanger used her conflict with the Church to portray birth control as a matter of American freedom is historian Kathleen Tobin. Both her doctoral dissertation, "Population and Power: The

---

[5]*The Mike Wallace Interview* (September 21, 1957), Harry Ransom Center: The University of Texas at Austin website, http://www.hrc.utexas-.edu/multimedia/video/2008/wallace/sanger_margaret.html   (accessed March 17, 2011).

[6]See especially, Ellen Chesler, *Woman of Valor: Margaret Sanger and the Birth Control Movement in America* (New York, Simon & Schuster, 1992). For a more laudatory account of Sanger's life, see Emily Taft Douglas, *Margaret Sanger: Pioneer of the Future* (New York: Holt, Rinehart and Winston, 1970). For a slightly more critical account, see David M. Kennedy, *Birth Control in America: The Career of Margaret Sanger* (New Haven: Yale University Press, 1970).

Religious Debate over Contraception, 1916–1936" and her book based upon it, *The American Religious Debate over Birth Control, 1907–1937,* clearly show Sanger's use of anti-Catholicism in her promotion of birth control. In these works, Tobin explains that "to aid in swaying the mainstream to support her, Sanger played upon middle-America's anti-Catholic sentiment. She repeatedly told Americans that the Church was not only a threat to her, but to them as well." Tobin further explains that Sanger "condemned the Church for infringing on her right to speak publicly, and accused the Catholic clergy of taking an antiquated position because they were unmarried and, therefore knew nothing of family life. Most importantly, she portrayed the Church as the only force working against her."[7]

Though Tobin's scholarship is thorough, there are some areas she does not fully explore. Most significantly, she does not show the extent to which Sanger was genuinely anti-Catholic and truly believed her birth control campaign was a revolution against the fixed moral structure of the Church. Rather, Tobin seems to suggest that Sanger chose to attack the Catholic Church because it was convenient and beneficial to do so. As Tobin explains, Sanger's socialist background taught her "the importance of identifying an enemy when initiating a social movement. After she had rejected socialism in her effort to gain mainstream support of her cause, she could benefit in identifying the Catholic Church as her enemy, as Catholics had already been marginalized."[8]

While it is probably true that these practical considerations influenced Sanger, and while the American anti-Catholic tradition definitely gave her much material to work with, her use of anti-Catholic propaganda was not merely a matter of

---

[7]Kathleen Tobin-Schlesinger, "Population and Power: The Religious Debate over Contraception, 1916–1936," (PhD diss., University of Chicago, 1994), 21.

[8]Kathleen A. Tobin, *The American Religious Debate over Birth Control, 1907–1937* (Jefferson, NC: McFarland and Company, 2001), 80.

expediency but rather stemmed from her anti-Catholic background and was a central part of her broader campaign for a new civilization based upon a pragmatic moral code.

CHAPTER 1

A BRIEF HISTORY OF
AMERICAN ANTI-CATHOLICISM

In order to fully understand the way Margaret Sanger used anti-Catholicism to carry out her birth control revolution, it is necessary to have some knowledge of both the origins of laws against birth control in the United States as well as some understanding of the history of American anti-Catholicism.[1] In regard to this first point, it is important to note that the original American laws against birth control were not instituted under Catholic pressure. Some scholars in fact argue that there may even have been an anti-Catholic motive in their passing. Among these is Alexander Sanger, grandson of Margaret Sanger, who is himself a passionate birth control advocate. Alexander Sanger attributes many of these laws to the greed of a newly professionalizing American medical community in the mid-to-late-nineteenth century. He sees anti-birth-control statutes as a tool which professionally trained physicians used to shut out unprofessional competitors, who often specialized in birth control services. Professional physicians were helped

---

[1]For a strongly pro-birth-control look at the background of anti-birth-control laws, see Angus McLaren, *A History of Contraception: From Antiquity to the Present Day* (Oxford: Basil Blackwell, 1990).

in their campaign against birth control, says Sanger, by members of an anti-Catholic organization, the Order of the Star Spangled Banner, who feared that Catholics were outbreeding Protestants because of Protestant birth control use. These practical reasons for outlawing birth control, claims Sanger, combined with an increasing Victorian morality, led to stringent anti-birth-control statutes, the most famous of which came from the federal Comstock Act of 1873.[2]

Anthony Comstock, a devout Congregationalist whose name was given to the famous nineteenth-century decency law, is often characterized in histories of the birth control movement as a sexual prude. Even if this description is a bit harsh, there can be no doubt that he was a zealous crusader for Victorian moral norms, as the name of his purity organization, the New York Society for the Suppression of Vice, attests. In 1873, Comstock convinced Congress to pass an anti-obscenity bill, which included prohibitions on the spread of birth control devices and information. So it was that the strongest legislation against birth control in the United States came about through Protestant rather than Catholic effort. As a United States Postal Inspector, Comstock became the chief enforcer of the new law, a position which brought him into direct confrontation with birth control advocates, including Margaret Sanger.[3]

For her part, Sanger resented Comstock and pilloried him in many of her writings, but he would not be her chief

---

[2]Alexander Sanger, *Beyond Choice: Reproductive Freedom in the 21st Century* (New York: PublicAffairs, 2004), 24–29. The Order of the Star Spangled Banner, more commonly known as the Know-Nothings, will be further explained later in this chapter. As far as moral reasons, Alexander Sanger attributes nineteenth-century prohibitions of birth control to "the feminist and fundamentalist drive for social purity in sexual matters."

[3]See Chapter 1 in Andrea Tone, *Devices and Desires: A History of Contraceptives in America* (New York: Hill and Wang, 2001). Tone also seems to agree with Alexander Sanger that the professionalization of medicine helped lead to laws against birth control.

opponent in the battle over birth control. That distinction belonged to the Catholic Church. Fortunately for Sanger, the Church had a long history of unpopularity in America, a situation which she could and did exploit. In order to understand how she accomplished this, it is helpful to know the extent to which anti-Catholicism was present in the United States throughout its history.

Historians have thoroughly documented the long-standing American tradition of anti-Catholicism. In his 1956 work, *American Catholicism*, Msgr. John Tracy Ellis relates a conversation he once had with Harvard professor Arthur M. Schlesinger Sr., during which Schlesinger told him, "I regard the prejudice against your Church as the deepest bias in the history of the American people."[4] There is no shortage of evidence to back up Schlesinger's statement.

Anti-Catholicism came to American shores with the first Protestant settlers and is visible in early colonial documents and events.[5] Even Maryland, a colony founded as a safe haven for Catholics, eventually became a hostile place as neighboring Protestants violently invaded and took control of the government there.[6] With the coming of the American Revolution, Catholics gained long-denied political and religious rights, though some states kept their established churches and continued to maintain political handicaps on Catholics. Even though American and French Catholic participation in the fight for American freedom had somewhat lessened the nation's anti-Catholic spirit, a lingering suspicion and animosity remained.[7]

---

[4]John Tracy Ellis, *American Catholicism* (Chicago: The University of Chicago Press, 1956), 149.

[5]For example, the charter granted to the Massachusetts Bay colony by William and Mary stated "that forever hereafter there shall be a Liberty of Conscience allowed in the worship of God to all Christians, except Papists." It should also be noted that the first religiously motivated Protestant settlers were the Puritans, who desired to purge their church of all things Catholic.

By the mid-nineteenth century, American anti-Catholicism was at its worst. Perhaps the most infamous example was the burning of the Ursaline convent in Charlestown, Massachusetts, in 1834. Such mob outrages were spurred on by a stream of anti-Catholic publications, the most recognized of which was Maria Monk's *Awful Disclosures of the Hotel Dieu Nunnery of Montreal*, published in 1836. Such blatantly false, highly sexualized literature became favorite reading for many Americans who were becoming increasingly interested in the supposed perversity of the Roman Catholic Church and in alleged Catholic subversion.[8] In 1849, Protestant fears of rapid Catholic immigration—and of the impending takeover of the country that would surely result—led to the formation of the

------

[6]Catholics in Maryland had always been in the minority and had done their best to practice their faith unobtrusively, but in 1645, during the English Civil War, Virginia Puritans under Richard Ingle attacked and ransacked the colony, plunging it into a state of anarchy. Catholics did not fare well during this invasion. As Jay Dolan explains, "Jesuit priests and Catholic leaders were led off to England in chains." To make matters even worse, a similar invasion occurred in 1654. Then, in 1689, in the wake of the Glorious Revolution, Maryland became a Protestant colony, and the religious toleration which had existed under the founding Calvert family ceased. The 1704 "Act to prevent the Growth of Popery within this Province" made it illegal for Catholic priests to try to win converts or say Mass. Catholics in the colony also lost their voting rights. Though these laws were not always enforced and were lightened as time went on, their very existence in a colony that was once Catholic shows the extent to which many Protestant colonists feared and hated "papists." See Jay Dolan, *The American Catholic Experience: A History from Colonial Times to the Present* (Garden City, NY: Image Books of Doubleday, 1987), 69–97.

[7]Thomas Jefferson demonstrated this lingering distrust in an 1814 letter to Horatio Spafford. "In every country and in every age," he said, "the priest has been hostile to liberty. He is always in alliance with the Despot abetting his abuses in return for protection of his own." Though Jefferson was not referring specifically to Catholic priests, it is clear this comment meant to include them, and that in his mind, they could never be counted on to support American democracy. The letter can be found at the Library of Congress American Memory website, www.memory.loc.gov.

Order of the Star Spangled Banner, more commonly known as
the Know-Nothings because of the evasive replies given by
members when questioned about their secret activities. The
Know-Nothings, fueling their campaigns with anti-immigrant
and anti-Catholic rhetoric, managed to gain significant political power at local and state levels.[9]

While the Know-Nothing party crumbled in the years
leading up to the Civil War, anti-Catholicism remained in
political propaganda about slavery and secession. The preoccupation of the nation with the war and emancipation left little
time for actual violence against Catholics, but the continued
anti-Catholic rhetoric, especially in the North, made many
Catholics fear that the Republican-controlled government
would turn on them once the South was defeated.[10] In 1887, a
group of conservative Protestants worried about continued
Catholic encroachments founded the American Protective
Association (APA), which quickly gained great popularity
through its use of hysterical and outrageous anti-Catholic propaganda.[11] Despite its immense popularity among conservative
Protestants in the 1890s, the APA quickly withered as its prin-

---

[8]James Hennesey, *American Catholics: A History of the Roman
Catholic Community in the United States*, paperback ed. (New York: Oxford
University Press, 1983), 121–22. The destruction of the convent was spurred
on by Rebecca Reed, who had written about her "experiences" with the
Ursalines and was in town stirring up trouble when the mob attacked. Also
present in the town was the notoriously anti-Catholic preacher Lyman
Beecher. Hennessey explains that none of the mob ever suffered any real
consequences for their actions even though the case was brought to trial.

[9]Jay P. Dolan, *The American Catholic Experience*, 202. For an
extended account of antebellum anti-Catholicism, see Jenny Franchot,
Roads to Rome: The Antebellum Protestant Encounter with Catholicism
(Berkeley, CA: University of California Press, 1994).

[10]John T. McGreevy, *Catholicism and American Freedom: A History* (New York: W.W. Norton, 2003), 75. Earlier, McGreevy explains why
this fear was not entirely unfounded in light of events happening elsewhere
in the world, especially as these events were being praised by Republicans.

ciples fell out of favor with mainstream America, and its bigotry came under increasing attack from liberal Protestants and
secular intellectuals. In addition, explains John McGreevy in
Catholicism and American Freedom, as the rampant abuses of
growing industry, powerful monopolies, and unbridled indi-
vidualism became more apparent toward the close of the century, some American reformers began looking at the social
teachings of the Catholic Church as possible answers to
America's problems.[12]

Even with these changes and a growing acceptance of
Catholicism taking place, American anti-Catholicism continued into the twentieth century, most visibly in the form of
yet another semi-secret organization, the second Ku Klux Klan,
which organized in 1915 and which eventually targeted
Catholics as its number-one enemy.[13] By the same year, the
fanatically anti-Catholic newspaper *The Menace* had a circula-
tion of 1.6 million copies per week.[14] Anti-Catholicism was not
limited to radical groups during this time, though. Fear of
Catholics found expression in the passage of a number of laws,
particularly at the state level. These included a 1919 Alabama

---

[11]Hennessey describes the depth of thought and level of honesty
found in the organization as he explains that "it achieved its greatest prominence in 1893 when the A.P.A. spread the rumor that a papal decree had
absolved all oaths of allegiance to the United States and that a massacre of
heretics was planned for September 5, which they mistakenly thought was
the feast day of St. Ignatius Loyola, founder of the Jesuit order." See Hennessey, *American Catholics*, 182–83.

[12]McGreevy, *Catholicism and American Freedom*, 126.

[13]John Higham, *Strangers in the Land: Patterns in American
Nativism* (New York: Atheneum, 1963), 291. Higham explains that anti-
Catholicism actually did not become a part of the Klan's platform until sev-
eral years after its founding.

[14]Justin Nordstrom, *Danger on the Doorstep: Anti-Catholicism
and American Print Culture in the Progressive Era* (Notre Dame: University
of Notre Dame Press, 2006), 10.

law which allowed warrantless searches of convents and a 1922 Oregon law that virtually banned Catholic schools in the state.[15] In 1928, Democrat Al Smith lost a presidential campaign during which southern Protestant ministers drew much negative attention to his Catholic religious affiliation, thereby convincing their congregations to vote against their traditional party.[16]

Despite Al Smith's defeat, the situation for American Catholics was improving in the early 1930s. Many Americans suffering through the Great Depression were receptive to the ideas laid out in Pope Pius XI's 1931 social justice encyclical *Quodragesimo Anno*. Some of the concepts presented in the encyclical even found their way into the early programs of Franklin D. Roosevelt's New Deal, a point of considerable pride for American Catholics. Because of this, and because Roosevelt granted Catholics important positions in his administration, many historians see the Roosevelt presidency as a turning point in the story of American anti-Catholicism.[17]

[15]Many Protestants and Jews opposed the Oregon law, which Hennessey explains was sponsored by Scottish Rite Masons. The Supreme Court declared the law unconstitutional in the 1925 case *Pierce v. Society of Sisters*. The Alabama convent inspection law was passed in response to continued fears of sexual depravity within convents, as sensationalized by the pornographic works of Maria Monk and others. For an interesting look at the culture which led to the law, see Sharon Davies, *Rising Road: A True Tale of Love, Race, and Religion in America* (Oxford: Oxford University Press, 2010).

[16]McGreevy, *Catholicism and American Freedom*, 150. For accounts of Al Smith's failed campaign, see Edmund A. Moore, *A Catholic Runs for President: The Campaign of 1928* (New York: The Ronald Press Company, 1956) and Allan J. Lichtman, *Prejudice and the Old Politics: The Presidential Election of 1928* (Chapel Hill, NC: University of North Carolina Press, 1979).

[17]George Q. Flynn argues that "it was under Franklin Roosevelt and the New Deal that American Catholics were given recognition as a major force in society and were raised to 'a new level of association . . . indicating a change in the 'official' American attitude toward the Church, and equally

As the twentieth century progressed, tolerance of Catholics seemed ever more on the rise. Cross-denominational cooperation on World War II battlefields significantly diminished Protestant fears of Catholics, and increasing interaction between Protestants and Catholics in the post-war suburbs furthered this trend.[18] In 1955, sociologist Will Herberg declared Catholicism to be one of the three great American religions in his landmark work *Protestant, Catholic, Jew: An Essay in American Religious Sociology.*

By the second half of the twentieth century, the time had come when a Catholic could again hope to gain the highest office in the land. This was precisely what happened with the election of John F. Kennedy, though Protestant resistance to his presidential campaign showed that many Americans still had reservations about Catholicism. Kennedy's electoral victory and subsequent failure to turn the nation over to the pope put many non-Catholics' fears to rest. As a result, a number of historians see the Kennedy presidency as the final nail in the coffin of American anti-Catholicism. This opinion, however, is still contested.[19]

While there is still debate among scholars over when, why, or even if American anti-Catholicism came to an end, most agree that it was once widespread, that it took on many different forms, and that it was used as propaganda for a wide

important, in the Church's disposition towards the government.'" Patrick Carey explains that Roosevelt elevated Catholics to "key administrative positions" in his government. Among these were such figures as Thomas Corcoran, Frank Murphy, and Joseph Kennedy. See George Q. Flynn, *American Catholics and the Roosevelt Presidency: 1932–36* (Lexington: University of Kentucky Press, 1968), xi; and, Patrick W. Carey, *Catholics in America: A History* (Westport, CT: Praeger, 2004), 88.

[18]Thomas T. McAvoy, *A History of the Catholic Church in the United States* (Notre Dame, IN: University of Notre Dame Press, 1969), 440. McAvoy explains that anti-Catholicism enjoyed a brief resurgence after WWII, but that it quickly died out because so many returning veterans had spent time with Catholics overseas and had discovered they were not so unlike other Americans.

variety of causes. Even early on, propagandists portrayed the Catholic Church as the enemy of free thought and free speech. In *Strangers in the Land*, John Higham explains that "since the Enlightenment, Americans had tended to look upon the Pope as a reactionary despot, hostile to liberty and progress alike."[20] Another historian, Justin Nordstrom, shows in his book, *Danger on the Doorstep: Anti-Catholicism and American Print Culture in the Progressive Era,* how rural anti-Catholic publications aroused hysteria with wild conspiracy theories of Catholic political subversion and arguments that Catholics could never be true Americans.[21] Finally, John McGreevy explains in *Catholicism and American Freedom* that in the late nineteenth and early twentieth centuries, a growing belief held that Catholicism hindered free thought and scientific progress. According to this theory, the Protestant Reformation had opened the door for the eventual embracing of free thought, while the Catholic Church continued to

---

[19]For an account of the many difficulties Kennedy faced as a Catholic running for the presidency, see Shaun A. Casey, *The Making of a Catholic President: Kennedy vs. Nixon, 1960* (New York: Oxford University Press, 2009).

[20]Higham, *Strangers in the Land*, 178–79. Among the popular historical anti-Catholic tropes Higham lists are "the moral iniquities of confessional and convent, warnings about Catholic political conspiracies [and] widespread rumors that the faithful were drilling nightly in church basements in preparation for an armed uprising."

[21]See Nordstrom, *Danger on the Doorstep.* Nordstrom demonstrates the way the editors of these publications, using extreme over-exaggeration and blatant falsehoods, appealed to the masculinity of conservative American Protestant men and urged them to resist the dangerous inroads being made by Rome. He explains, "Anti-Catholic texts proved popular in the 1910s because their writers both evoked traditional anti-Catholic tropes that had a proven track record of notoriety and financial success and used these popular tropes to address pressing social and cultural concerns in the early twentieth century."

oppress such freedom wherever Church authorities still had power.[22]

Historical anti-Catholicism is perhaps best summarized by Philip Jenkins in *The New Anti-Catholicism: The Last Acceptable Prejudice*. In this work, Jenkins argues that while at certain times anti-Catholicism has received less attention than at others, it has long existed as an undercurrent in American thought. He explains:

> The power of anti-Catholicism lies in its infinite adaptability. In different times and places, different kinds of anti-papist rhetoric have been more in evidence, but none has entirely vanished from view. Each is ready to rise again when it meets the needs of a particular political movement or interest group.[23]

Jenkins's theory that special interests readily used anti-Catholicism to promote their causes certainly holds true in the case of Margaret Sanger and the birth control movement. Sanger was quite adept at using American anti-Catholicism to advance the acceptance of birth control. She exploited many of the themes just mentioned, particularly that of alleged Catholic opposition to liberty and science. By portraying her struggle for birth control as a fight for these principles against Catholic tyranny, she sought to convince non-Catholic Americans to embrace her movement. Sanger's use of anti-Catholicism, however, was not merely a matter of convenience. As the next

---

[22]McGreevy, *Catholicism and American Freedom*, 102–4. As evidence of this, McGreevy cites such works as Emile de Laveleye's *Protestantism and Catholicism, in Their Bearing upon the Liberty and Prosperity of Nations* and Max Weber's *Protestant Ethic and the Spirit of Capitalism*.

[23]Philip Jenkins, *The New Anti-Catholicism: The Last Acceptable Prejudice* (Oxford: Oxford University Press, 2003), 45. Among various types of anti-Catholic tropes, Jenkins lists the sexual perversion of confessionals, convents, and celibacy; the brainwashing occurring in Catholic education; and the Catholic reputation for deception, duplicity, and intrigue. Ultimately, he argues that anti-Catholicism is alive and well in modern pop culture.

chapter will demonstrate, both she and the birth control movement were intimately connected with hostility to the Catholic
Church from the very beginning.

CHAPTER 2

THE MOVEMENT'S RADICAL ROOTS

To fully understand the way Margaret Sanger and birth control were diametrically opposed to Catholic influence in America, one must look at the early, tangled roots of the American birth control movement. From the start, birth control was associated with a number of radical leftist causes.[1] In *The Moral Veto: Framing Contraception, Abortion, and Cultural Pluralism in the United States*, Gene Burns points out and explains the intimate links between the birth control movement and the American socialist and feminist movements. Of these and other radical causes of the time, he says, "It was often difficult to see where one cause ended and another began. . . . It was almost impossible to discuss birth control, or any single issue, independently of the morally charged mélange of leftist causes." Burns further explains that while most radical movements did not greatly emphasize birth control, its association with radicalism helped fortify conservative

---

[1]The word "radical" means "to change at the root" and can refer to any kind of drastic or fundamental transformation. In this work, however, the terms "radicals" and "radicalism" will be used to describe a number of leftist causes at the turn of the century, from free love to anarchism. The terms will often be used more or less interchangeably with socialists and socialism.

energy against it.[2] Sanger only strengthened birth control's image as a component of radicalism when, for the masthead of her first paper, the *Woman Rebel*, she took the slogan "No Gods, No Masters" from the Industrial Workers of the World.[3]

In the nineteenth and early twentieth centuries, the Catholic Church served as a great hindrance to the success of many radical causes, proving itself a powerful and determined enemy. The late nineteenth-century popes strongly and repeatedly condemned socialism, communism, and other forms of political radicalism. As early as 1849, Pope Pius IX complained of the "wicked theories" and "perverted teachings" of socialism and communism.[4] Pope Leo XIII condemned both systems in his 1881 encyclical *Diuturnum* and again in his 1884 *Humanum Genus*. Even earlier, in 1878, he foreshadowed the debate to come when he accused socialists and other radicals of subverting the natural family, saying they "debase the natural union of man and woman, which is held sacred even among barbarous peoples; and its bond, by which the family is chiefly held together, they weaken, or even deliver up to lust."[5] Roman condemnations of this kind continued well into the twentieth century, drawing the battle lines between Catholic authority and leftist radicalism.

Papal pronouncements in and of themselves should not have created much obstruction to radical endeavors in a largely Protestant nation on the other side of the Atlantic

---

[2]Gene Burns, *The Moral Veto: Framing Contraception, Abortion, and Cultural Pluralism in the United States* (New York: Cambridge University Press, 2005), 30, 52.

[3]Alexander Sanger, *Beyond Choice*, 33. The Industrial Workers of the World or IWW (whose members were often referred to as "Wobblies") was a radical trade union which included many anarchists and socialists among its first members. One of the organization's first leaders was "Big Bill" Haywood, a close friend of Margaret Sanger.

[4]Pius IX, *Nostis et Nobiscum*, December 8, 1849, in Papal Encyclicals Online, http://www.papalencyclicals.net/Pius09/p9nostis.htm (accessed January 17, 2011).

Ocean, except for the fact that many of the lower-class masses the radicals were trying to sway were largely Catholic. The Catholic Church's hierarchical structure allowed for the systematic distribution of papal teachings among these lower classes. This greatly frustrated efforts by radicals to "convert" Catholic laborers. John McGreevy explains that in cities such as New York and Milwaukee, embittered socialist organizers complained that Catholic priests prevented their flocks from joining the socialist union ranks. In response, he says, socialists launched fierce attacks on the Church, further dividing Catholic and radical forces.[6]

The anarchist social agitator Emma Goldman was perhaps one of the best examples of the enmity that existed between leftist radicalism and Catholicism at the turn of the century. While her disdain for all organized religion was well known, she leveled some especially strong attacks at the Catholic hierarchy. A prime example of her penchant for anti-Catholic diatribes can be found in a eulogy she wrote for the revolutionary Catalan educator Francisco Ferrer, founder of the radical Modern School system, after he was executed by the Spanish government in 1909.[7] In that article, she lambasted the Church's secret, behind-the-scenes dealings and its

---

[5]Leo XIII, *Diuturnum*, June 29, 1881. Vatican: The Holy See. http://www.vatican.va/holy_father/leo_xiii/encyclicals/documents/hf_lxiii _enc_29061881_diuturnum_en.html (accessed January 17, 2011); Leo XIII, *Humanum Genus*, April 20, 1884. Vatican: The Holy See. http://www.vatican.va/holy_father/leo_xiii/encyclicals/documents/hf_l-xiii_enc_18840420 _humanum-genus_en.html (accessed January 17, 2011); Leo XIII, *Quod Apostolici Muneris*, December 28, 1878, in Papal Encyclicals Online. http://www.papalencyclicals.net/Leo13/l13apost.htm (accessed January 17, 2011). Papal encyclicals, according to the Catholic Encyclopedia, are "circulating letters ... explicitly addressed to the patriarchs, primates, archbishops, and bishops of the Universal Church in communion with the Apostolic See."

[6]John T. McGreevy, *Catholicism and American Freedom: A History* (New York: W.W. Norton, 2003), 145.

oppression of all free thought, referring to "the hideousness of that black monster, the Catholic Church." She declared her affinity for European revolutionary leaders whose campaigns were directed "not merely against the overthrow of despotism, but particularly against the Catholic Church, which from its very inception has been the enemy of all progress and liberalism."[8] Goldman was a perfect embodiment of the conflict between radicals and Catholics in the United States, a fact which is especially significant because of her role as one of the earliest American advocates of birth control.

It is evident that the early roots of the American birth control movement were intimately entangled with those of other radical causes, which in turn were irreconcilably opposed to the Catholic Church. Like the movement she came to lead, Margaret Sanger herself hailed from a thoroughly radical and anti-Catholic background. In retrospect, it seems almost impossible for her not to have come into conflict with the Church. She once explained that she had been "rocked in the

---

[7]Goldman paints a rather benign picture of Ferrer, which only serves to highlight her radicalism and anti-Catholicism. In actuality, Ferrer had once been arrested for participating in an anti-government uprising, and his school system sought to promote not only atheism (a serious offense in a nation that did not practice separation of church and state), but revolutionary sentiments as well.

[8]Emma Goldman, "Francisco Ferrer and the Modern Schools," in *Anarchism and Other Essays*, 3rd rev. ed. (New York: Mother Earth Publishing Association, 1917), in The Emma Goldman Papers, http://sunsite.berkeley.edu/goldman/Writings/Anarchism/ferrer.html   (accessed December 16, 2011). Goldman also played upon the theme of clerical sexual depravity. She criticized Catholic newspapers for claiming that Ferrer had a sexual relation with a rich woman in order to inherit her money for his school program and launched a counterattack, saying, "Of course, those who know the purity of the Catholic clergy will understand the insinuation. Have the Catholic priests ever looked upon woman as anything but a sex commodity?" She continued, "The historical data regarding the discoveries in the cloisters and monasteries will bear me out in that. How, then, are they to understand the co-operation of a man and a woman, except on a sex basis?"

cradle of socialism," and it is apparent that she was just as surely brought up in a strong tradition of anti-Catholicism.[9]

Margaret Sanger's exposure to radicalism and anti-Catholicism came very early in life. She was born in the glass-manufacturing town of Corning, New York, in 1879 to Irish working-class parents. While biographers describe her mother, Anne Purcell, as a devout Catholic, they also relate that she refrained from attending Mass in order to please her husband, Michael Higgins, whose aversion to the Catholic Church was well known in the strongly Catholic community. While Higgins despised Catholicism, his work as a stonecutter often relied on contracts making tombstones for the local Catholic cemetery. As Sanger herself explained it, "the Catholics were his best patrons, but he did not agree with Catholicism. He resented its clutch upon the human mind, its intolerance of reason, its abject subservience to Rome. He argued and debated on the side of reason, and influenced other men to resent the interference of the Church with progress of the mind."[10]

Higgins's cantankerous spirit and longing for passionate debate soon led him into serious trouble and cost him his livelihood. While he had never been a particularly good worker, often preferring to spend his time drinking and arguing with customers, it was a direct confrontation with local Catholic authorities that led to his and his family's financial ruin, a fact which could not have increased the love of Catholicism in the hearts of his family members. Always the supporter of progressive social causes, Higgins had invited the atheist and anti-clerical reformer Robert Ingersoll to come give a lecture in the strongly Irish-Catholic town. This did not please the

---

[9]Margaret Sanger, "Fabian Hall Speech" draft, July 5, 1915, in The Public Writings and Speeches of Margaret Sanger, http://www.nyu.edu/projects/sanger/webedition/app/documents/show. php ? Sanger Doc=128066.xml (accessed December 14, 2010). (Hereafter abbreviated as PWS.)

[10]Margaret Sanger, *My Fight for Birth Control* (New York: Farrar and Rinehart, 1931), 6.

local churchmen or parishioners. The parish priest who owned the hall at which Ingersoll was supposed to speak refused to let his building be used for such purposes, and as Sanger proudly related the story years later, a crowd of angry townspeople drove her father and Ingersoll away, forcing them instead to have their meeting out in a wooded area.[11]

In Sanger's young mind, her father was a hero for standing up to Church authorities, angry parishioners, and their alleged rejection of free speech. This apparently left quite an impression on her. According to Sanger and her biographers, Higgins was a strong influence on her life and on her later ideology. She recounted that despite his failings, "he . . . was fearless in mental battles, and it was from him that I learned the value of freedom of speech and personal liberty."[12]

Even without the Ingersoll incident, it is evident that Sanger was growing up in an atmosphere with little respect for the faith of her mother. In *My Fight for Birth Control*, she recalled an instance in her childhood when her father questioned her saying the Lord's Prayer verbatim, "devastating" her, but also waking up her mind. "I began to reason for myself," she said, "and it was disturbing. But my father had taught me to think."[13]

---

[11]Sanger, *My Fight for Birth Control*, 7. Also see Margaret Sanger, *An Autobiography* (1938; repr., New York: Dover Publications, 1971). Whether Sanger, Higgins, and Ingersoll were really forced to leave the hall amidst a shower of rotten vegetables as Sanger recalled is a matter for debate. Ellen Chesler explains that Ingersoll's biographer tells of his visit to Corning, but not of this incident. Chesler says that Sanger, in telling her life story, was not always honest with the details. "Autobiography was for Margaret Sanger a wholly self-conscious gesture. . . . [S]he had patience for the particulars of her own past only to the extent that they formed a pattern and offered a compelling explanation for her life's work. To this end, the stories she told about herself may be more reliable as myth than as fact—facts were there for embellishment." See Chesler, *Woman of Valor*, 21–22.

[12]Sanger, *My Fight for Birth Control*, 6–8.

[13]Sanger, *My Fight for Birth Control*, 6–8.

It is true that Sanger's father encouraged her free thought, but what exactly did he teach her to think about? He wanted all of his many children to question dogma, but not all of his instruction involved making them doubt. He had his heroes, and he shared them with his family. Among these was the radical reformer Henry George, whose single-tax crusade brought the Catholic hierarchy down upon him and his ally, Fr. Edward McGlynn, both of whom exhibited vehement opposition to the Church's stance on social issues.[14] Higgins was such an admirer of these men that he named one of his children Henry George McGlynn in their honor. Thus it was that the Higgins children were weaned on stories of radical leaders struggling for liberty against the Catholic Church.[15]

The radical and anti-Catholic influences that played such a prominent role in Sanger's childhood continued to guide her as a young adult. She attended school for nursing and married an architect, William Sanger, with whom she had three children. The couple moved to New York City where they joined the local socialist party and frequently associated with such prominent radical figures as Upton Sinclair, Mabel Dodge, 'Big Bill' Haywood, and of course, Emma Goldman, who was instrumental in setting Sanger on her birth control crusade.[16] In early 1914, the Sangers toured Europe, visiting radicals there who would greatly influence Margaret's thought on birth control. Among these were the fantastically anti-Catholic Marie Stopes, as well as the famed sexologist, Havelock Ellis.[17]

---

[14]For an account of the American Catholic hierarchy's disputes with George and McGlynn, see McGreevy, *Catholicism and American Freedom*, 136–37.

[15]Higgins would read George's famous work, *Poverty and Progress*, to his children. As Lawrence Lader describes the sessions, "he would roar with delight at each meaty passage and make the children reread them – 'to elevate the mind.'" See Lawrence Lader, *The Margaret Sanger Story and the Fight for Birth Control* (Garden City, NY: Doubleday & Company, 1955), 14.

Sanger returned to Europe in October 1914 after fleeing the United States while facing prosecution for distributing obscene literature in the form of her publication *The Woman Rebel*. For disputed reasons, she came back from this and subsequent educational trips to Europe less openly enflamed with the socialist cause and more devoted solely to birth control.[18] Still, even as she placed her sympathy for other radical causes

---

[16]"Biographical Sketch," The Margaret Sanger Papers Project, http://www.nyu.edu/projects/sanger/secure/aboutms/index.html (accessed December 14, 2010); Chesler, *Woman of Valor*, 58, 86–87. Chesler explains Sanger's intimate relationship and mutual respect with Haywood of IWW fame. She further relates that while Sanger learned a great deal about birth control from Goldman, the two did not get along well on a personal level.

[17]Marie Stopes, a leading British birth control advocate, had an "anti-Catholic mania" according to her biographer, June Rose. She believed God had appeared to her and given her the mission of promoting birth control. Another biographer, Ruth Hall, says that she was obsessed with the idea of a secret Catholic plot against her. Hall quotes her as saying, "I am out for a much greater thing than birth control. I am out to smash the tradition of organized Christianity, and to enthrone Christ's own tradition of wholesome, healthy, natural love towards sex life." See June Rose, *Marie Stopes and the Sexual Revolution* (London: Faber and Faber, 1992), 193; Ruth Hall, *Passionate Crusader: The Life of Marie Stopes* (New York: Harcourt Brace Jovanovich, 1977), 260. Henry Havelock Ellis (1859–1939) was a British pioneer in the study of human sexuality whose works openly challenged contemporary sexual values, including in the fields of homosexuality and transgenderism.

[18]"Biographical Sketch," The Margaret Sanger Papers Project; Kevin E. McClearey, "'A Tremendous Awakening': Margaret H. Sanger's Speech at Fabian Hall," *Western Journal of Communication*, 58 (Summer 1994), 183–84; Chelser, *Woman of Valor*, 57. Some scholars, such as Linda Gordon, argue that Sanger was influenced by her British and European counterparts to tone down her radical rhetoric and present her birth control efforts as part of a respectable movement. David Kennedy supports this view, especially emphasizing the influence Havelock Ellis had on her. Joan M. Jensen, on the other hand, says that though the influence of European friends may have been partially responsible for Sanger's shying away from

in the background, Sanger maintained her animosity toward the Catholic Church, a fact revealed in many of her writings.

Given her radical background, it is not surprising that Sanger, like Goldman, loudly and strongly protested the execution of the radical Spanish educator Francisco Ferrer and blamed it primarily on the Catholic Church. In a harshly-worded article on the subject, she accused the Church of being antithetical to democracy and due process of law. She declared that the memory of Ferrer's death "burns in the hearts of his comrades like a cankered wound, and shall continue to embitter their lives until those they know responsible for his death shall have been called to account." She hoped and believed this revenge would come swiftly. "Spain," she said, "is one of the last countries to continue in the clutches of the Church of Rome, and even here one can feel the ebbing tide of its downfall by the attitude of the people who sneer and joke at the priests in passing, to say nothing of the convents and churches burned and demolished by the people each time there is an uprising." To make it clear that she was not merely stating the facts, but was actually condoning action against the Church, she explained, "The first awakening and forward step of Spain will be to drive the priests out of the country as was done in France only a few years ago."[19]

The account Sanger gave of Ferrer's death reveals her deep-seated hatred for the Catholic Church and also demonstrates her ability to use dramatic rhetoric against it, as she accused it of inculcating "superstition" and of brutally sup-

radical socialism, she mostly chose this course in light of the changing U.S. political climate during World War I and the post-war period. She describes the crackdowns on leftist organizations during this period and the unfeasibility of relying on their support for birth control, explaining, "Sanger may have continued to work with the American Left had political circumstances been otherwise." Kevin E. McClearey attributes Sanger's change to the poor reaction she undoubtedly received for her radical speech at Fabian Hall in 1915. Vanessa Murphree and Karla K. Gower see Sanger as having remained a radical until 1929 when she legitimized birth control by helping establish the National Committee on Federal Legislation for Birth Control.

pressing "the teachings of freedom, truth and reason" in an attempt to defeat its great enemy, "the facts of natural science and evolution."[20] From the beginning, then, both Sanger and the birth control movement were closely connected with radicalism and with a strident anti-Catholic spirit. Sanger's later use of anti-Catholic rhetoric in the promotion of birth control was not merely a matter of convenience, but rather came naturally to her from her radical, anti-Catholic background. Nevertheless, she soon realized it was advantageous to exploit latent anti-Catholic fears in America, and she did so with great gusto, portraying her campaign for birth control as a fight for American freedom against the dark oppression of the Catholic Church.

---

[19]Margaret Sanger, "Modern Schools in Spain," *The Modern School* (May 1916): 5–9, in PWS, http://www.nyu.edu/projects/sanger/-webedition/app/documents/show.php?sangerDoc=320329.xml (accessed December 14, 2010). The image of burned convents and churches was nothing new to the American people. Sanger's description of the expulsion of priests as a "forward step" hearkened back to the days when Jesuits were banned from various American colonies under pain of death. Her description of "the clutches of the Church of Rome" was indicative of the belief that the Catholic Church exercised its secret influence to control the political and social institutions of nations.

[20]Sanger, "Modern Schools in Spain," 5–9.

CHAPTER 3

EARLY RHETORIC AND
THE TOWN HALL INCIDENT

In a 1916 article entitled "Birth Control," Margaret Sanger laid out the fact that her birth control campaign was a call for a moral revolution. She also indicated her belief that the Catholic Church would be her principle opponent in the years to come. From the first lines of her article, she set up her struggle as a crusade for moral freedom and connected it with the American revolutionary tradition, proclaiming, "We in the United States are entering upon a fight for moral liberty, much as our parents entered the fight for political and religious liberty in the past."[1]

There was nothing unusual about Sanger connecting her movement with the tradition of the American Revolution. Many progressive causes had done the same thing in the past. Abolitionists had used this type of language in their fight against slavery, and the women's rights movement had sym-

---

[1]Margaret Sanger, "Birth Control," *The Melting Pot* (July 1916): 5–6, in PWS, http://www.nyu.edu/projects/sanger/webedition/app/documents/show.php?sangerDoc=303217.xml (accessed December 14, 2010).

bolically plagiarized the Declaration of Independence in a call for the liberation of women at Seneca Falls in 1848. It was only natural for Sanger to appeal to American patriotic sentiment with such language, and she continued to do this as her article progressed. "Freedom in political, religious and moral thought," she explained, "are absolutely essential to the progress of every civilized country. We have fought for freedom for the first and second, but the third has been slumbering and we have not awakened it."[2]

With this last segment, Sanger made it clear she intended to cross a line not taken by earlier movements. While the abolition and women's rights movements had demanded that various American freedoms and rights be shared by all, Sanger was calling for a revolution of morality itself. She was advocating what she would later describe as a "new morality," though the expression was not uniquely hers. She complained that "public censors" were doing their utmost to maintain the older moral structure and prevent the discussion of birth control. At this time she still categorized a wide variety of organizations as the enemies of her movement,[3] but even now she began pointing her finger at the Catholic Church specifically:

> Take the clergy, (Catholics especially). They are the beneficiaries of the church that has made breeding its main source of revenue. They preach from a "sacred book" to "multiply and replenish the earth," knowing that large families among working people tend to preserve their influence and authority. They tell us that every baby is a

---

[2]Sanger, "Birth Control," 5–6.

[3]Other opponents Sanger complained of at this time were doctors, politicians, industrialists, and militants. Gene Burns explains how she managed to bring the medical profession around to her side and successfully present birth control as a medical issue. See Chapter 3 in Gene Burns, *The Moral Veto: Framing Contraception, Abortion, and Cultural Pluralism in the United States* (New York: Cambridge University Press, 2005).

new soul presented to God, and for his glory and honor women must produce as many souls as possible.[4]

While at this point Sanger lamented "the miserable threats of priests and preachers," it is apparent that she was already beginning to point to the Catholic Church as the chief religious opponent of birth control. While this would in short time be an accurate description, it was not quite true at this earlier period. Historian Leslie Tentler has shown that prior to 1920, most Catholic priests were reluctant to condemn birth control, either from the pulpit or in the confessional, out of fear of scandalizing those who did not yet know of such things. She also explains that some of the strongest condemnations of birth control during these early years came from conservative Anglicans and Lutherans, as well as from Catholics.[5] A few years later, Sanger would be more justified in claiming Catholics as her chief opponents, but her use of this claim at this early period belies a preconceived notion of the Catholic Church as the primary enemy of her birth control revolution.

It was not long before Sanger expanded her theory that the Catholic Church was her main religious adversary to include accusations that it was influencing the government against her. In October 1916, she intentionally violated New York state law by opening the Brownsville birth control clinic in Brooklyn, New York. The clinic remained open little more than a week before a female vice detective infiltrated it, leading

---

[4]Sanger, "Birth Control,"5–6. On the matter of clergy making revenue from a large number of births, Emily Taft Douglas, in her biography of Sanger (which is based heavily on Sanger's own questionable recounting of her life story) describes the story of one poor woman who came to Sanger for family limitation help, explaining that "the priest had told her to have many babies. . . . She had fifteen only six of whom lived, but the priest had made money on fifteen baptismal fees, nine funerals, masses and candles for the little ones." See Douglas, *Pioneer of the Future*, 106.

[5]Leslie Tentler, "'The Abominable Crime of Onan'": Catholic Pastoral Practice and Family Limitation in the United States, 1875–1919," *Church History* 71, no. 2 (June 2002): 315–16, 322.

to a police raid. The police arrested Sanger and imprisoned her, but she was shortly thereafter released. She promptly went back to the clinic and was just as promptly rearrested. [6] After this, she faced an uphill battle in the courts. In January 1918, the New York Court of Appeals found her guilty of violating state obscenity laws.[7] In the spring of that year, she wrote an article describing the Brownsville incident. While she noted the role of the Protestant Comstock authorities in the case, she placed much greater emphasis on the supposed role of the hidden Catholic influence in the prosecution:

> All the forces of opposition were on hand to malign individuals and to misrepresent the cause. The influence of the Roman Catholic Church was seen everywhere. ... Comstock's successor was also present to represent the "Society for the Suppression of Vice," but everywhere, and at every turn, the strongest opposition came from subtle underground workings of that Church which apparently dominates American courts of justice and political life today.[8]

This passage makes it apparent that Sanger was not only suggesting that the Catholic Church was the main opponent of birth control, but was playing anti-Catholic fears to their full potential. For decades, non-Catholic Americans had worried about the growing influence of the Church in Amer-

---

[6]Douglas, *Pioneer of the Future*, 105–10.

[7]Chesler, *Woman of Valor*, 159–160. The court did rule that birth control could be distributed by physicians for medical reasons. This would become an important precedent in later birth control cases which further eroded the Comstock laws. At the time it did not help Sanger, because she was not a physician.

[8]Margaret Sanger, "Clinics, Courts and Jails," *Birth Control Review* (April 1918): 3, in PWS, http://www.nyu.edu/projects/sanger/webedition/app/documents/show.php?sangerDoc=236476.xml (accessed December 14, 2010).

ican politics. Sanger now announced that the Catholic Church had managed to manipulate the American system of government and was actively using its control to smother the freedoms of everyday Americans by forcing its oppressive and unenlightened doctrines upon them.

The Catholic Church was quickly becoming, in Sanger's propaganda, the main enemy of her birth control movement, but it was not enough that the Church opposed birth control. In order to portray the matter as a case of the Church restricting the freedoms of Americans, Sanger needed to show that birth control was something Americans truly wanted. For this purpose, she repeatedly emphasized that there was a large demand for birth control. Her writings are replete with stories of poor, overburdened women of all faiths approaching her for information on limiting their families. By telling these stories, Sanger hoped to show that popular opinion was in favor of birth control. While this popular opinion made birth control perfectly legitimate in her new moral system, it also allowed her to contrast American democracy with Catholic moral absolutism, strengthening the image of the fight for birth control as a fight for American freedom.

By the late 1910s, it was no longer Sanger's imagination that the Catholic Church strongly and openly opposed her birth control movement. One of her most active opponents was Fr. John A. Ryan, a native of Minnesota and a prominent graduate of Catholic University of America in Washington, D.C. On most issues, Ryan actually had a reputation as a social progressive, and he was highly involved in causes related to just treatment of the working class.[9] Despite his liberal stance on many social issues, Ryan drew a hard line when it came to birth control, and some historians believe his efforts pressured the American bishops to openly do the same.[10] In September 1919,

---

[9]John T. McGreevy, *Catholicism and American Freedom: A History* (New York: W.W. Norton, 2003), 144.

[10]McGreevy, *Catholicism and American Freedom*, 158; Tentler, "The Abominable Crime of Onan," 338–39.

the bishops issued their first public statement against birth control:

> It is idealism of the truest and most practical sort that sees in marriage the divinely appointed plan for cooperating with the Creator in perpetuating the race, and that accepts the responsibility of bringing children into the world, who may prove either a blessing or a curse to society at large. Where such ideals prevail, the fulfillment of marital duties occasions no hardship. Neither is there any consideration for the fraudulent prudence that would purify life by defiling its source. The selfishness which leads to race suicide, with or without the pretext of bettering the species, is, in God's sight, "a detestable thing." It is the crime of individuals for which, eventually, the nation must suffer.[11]

With this statement, the American Catholic bishops not only condemned the practice of birth control, but also affirmed the Church's interest in preventing its use even in a largely non-Catholic society. Furthermore, they took a strong stand against the new morality, arguing that the commands of God trumped social problems, and that society could not hope to better itself by eugenic or other means if the practice of those means violated the laws of God. On the contrary, the bishops declared, such actions, even on the part of individuals, would

---

[11]"Pastoral Letter of the Archbishops and Bishops of the United States Assembled in Conference at the Catholic University of America, September 1919," (Washington, DC: The National Catholic Welfare Conference, 1920), 51–52. "A detestable thing" is a reference to the biblical story of Onan, which is parenthetically cited in the original pastoral letter. In the story, God commanded Onan to raise up a son for his deceased brother by marrying his widow, Tamar, in accordance with his leviratical duty. "But," says Scripture, "Onan knew that the heir would not be his; and it came to pass, when he went in to his brother's wife, that he emitted on the ground, lest he should give an heir to his brother. And the thing which he did displeased the LORD; therefore He killed him also." (Gen. 38:6–10, NKJV) Theologians have debated whether Onan was killed for his practice of withdrawal or whether God punished him for cheating his brother's widow of a child.

only lead to the degradation and eventual ruin of society. Such language clearly expressed the Catholic view of the importance of building civilization on the unchanging moral principles of natural law. Nothing could have been more opposed to the new morality and new civilization Sanger increasingly advocated.

Even though the Catholic Church was becoming an ever more outspoken opponent of birth control during this time, it did not stand alone in its opposition to Sanger's principles, as events in 1920 showed. That year, the Lambeth Conference of the Anglican Church issued a resolution on birth control that demonstrated a stance similar to that taken by the American Catholic bishops. The resolution showed that though birth control may have been growing in popularity among individuals, powerful institutional opposition still existed, especially in religious bodies. "While declining to lay down rules which [would] meet the needs of every abnormal case," the Lambeth Conference declared:

> We utter an emphatic warning against the use of unnatural means for the avoidance of conception, together with the grave dangers - physical, moral and religious - thereby incurred, and against the evils with which the extension of such use threatens the race . . . we steadfastly uphold what must always be regarded as the governing considerations of Christian marriage. One is the primary purpose for which marriage exists, namely the continuation of the race through the gift and heritage of children; the other is the paramount importance in married life of deliberate and thoughtful self-control.[12]

Despite Sanger's previous attempts to portray the Catholic Church as the chief opponent of birth control, the 1920 Lambeth statement shows that other influential religious groups were also hostile to her crusade. In 1921, though, she received an excellent tool for propaganda which she did not

---

[12]Lambeth Conference 1920, Resolution 68, "Problems of Marriage and Sexual Morality," http://www.lambethconference.org/resolutions/1920/1920–68.cfm (accessed March 8, 2011).

fail to exploit to the fullest. In November of that year, she arranged for the First American Birth Control Conference to take place at New York City's Town Hall. The conference schedule included a forum tellingly entitled, "Birth Control: Is It Moral?" The meeting agenda also listed talks by several prominent birth control advocates, including Sanger herself, but when the speakers and crowds arrived at the hall, the police were waiting for them. The officers grudgingly let them pass inside, but when Sanger tried to address the meeting, the police placed her and the other speakers under arrest. Some of the officers claimed they were sent to the meeting by New York's Archbishop Patrick Hayes, and the presence of Hayes's secretary, Msgr. Joseph Dineen, only gave further credence to these rumors.[13]

While Hayes did not acknowledge sending the police, the evidence for this theory appeared strong. Whether he actually played a part in the affair was irrelevant to Sanger, who seized the opportunity as evidence that the Catholic hierarchy was controlling the city government of New York and was using its power to suppress her free speech and force its moral code on American citizens. Non-Catholic Americans had, to varying degrees, feared this possibility for generations. Now, proclaimed Sanger, this nightmarish scenario had come true.

A week after the New York Town Hall incident, Sanger gave a speech entitled "The Morality of Birth Control" in which she openly accused Hayes. The title of the speech indicated that the question posed at the forum, "Birth Control: Is it Moral?" had been settled by the disruption of the meeting. In her speech, Sanger declared her conviction "that the discussion of the moral issue was one which did not solely belong to theologians and to scientists, but belonged to the people." In doing this, she not only reemphasized her belief in the new morality, but also placed herself on the side of democracy, in opposition to moral absolutism. She explained that in order to

---

[13]Kathleen Tobin-Schlesinger, "Population and Power: The Religious Debate over Contraception, 1916–1936," (PhD diss., University of Chicago, 1994), 80–81.

aid the public discussion on birth control, she had sent letters to different theologians asking their opinions on the matter. All had shown their belief in the democratic discussion of morality, she claimed, except for the Catholics. As she described it, "Every one who answered did so with sincerity and courtesy, with the exception of one group whose reply to this important question as demonstrated at the Town Hall last Sunday evening was a disgrace to liberty-loving people, and to all traditions we hold dear in the United States."[14]

Sanger's warnings of Catholic political power and her connections of birth control with American freedom reached a high point in an article she wrote for the December issue of her *Birth Control Review*. In that article, Sanger emphatically announced that the American Catholic hierarchy was conspiring behind the scenes to suppress all discussion of birth control and force Catholic morality upon every American citizen. She proclaimed that while the Church had been accused "thousands of times" of trying to subvert American freedom, it had been "caught in the act" with the suppression of the Town Hall meeting. She called on all non-Catholic Americans to resist the encroachments of the Church by embracing birth control as a matter of American freedom:

> All who resent this sinister Church Control of life and conduct–this interference of the Roman Church in attempting to dictate the conduct and behavior of non-Catholics, must now choose between Church Control or Birth Control. You can no longer remain neutral. You must make a declaration of independence, of self-reliance, or submit to the dictatorship of the Roman Catholic hierarchy.[15]

Sanger was obviously trying to exploit the publicity of the Town Hall incident to the fullest. It is difficult to say how

---

[14]Margaret Sanger, "The Morality of Birth Control," published speech (New York, 1921), in PWS, http://www.nyu.edu/projects/sanger/webedition/app/documents/show.php?sangerDoc=238254.xml (accessed December 14, 2010).

the general public responded to her announcement that they must all embrace and support birth control as a matter of American freedom, but the newspapers quickly picked up on her rhetoric. Kathleen Tobin explains that immediately following the incident, most media outlets sided with the police against Sanger, accusing her of being a troublemaker, but that by December opinions had changed, and Sanger found the press very supportive. The *Birth Control Review* for that month included an article entitled "The Press Protests," which was a compilation of various newspaper stories decrying the police interference with the birth control meeting. Attitudes on at least the public discussion of birth control were changing in Sanger's favor, and as she realized this, she declared that the Town Hall incident "will become celebrated in history as the great turning point in public opinion."[16]

---

[15]Margaret Sanger, "Church Control?" *Birth Control Review* 5, no. 12 (December 1921): 3–4, in *Birth Control Review* (New York: Da Capo Press, 1970).

[16]"The Press Protests," *Birth Control Review* 5, no. 12 (December 1921): 16–17, in *Birth Control Review* (New York: Da Capo Press, 1970).

CHAPTER 4

SANGER'S RHETORIC INTENSIFIES

Margaret Sanger lost no time exploiting the 1921 Town Hall affair to the fullest possible extent. What had begun as an apparent setback for her and the birth control movement had in a short time become a significant asset. The disruption of her birth control meeting by the police gave her a powerful propaganda tool to use against the Catholic Church, and she did not waste this opportunity. Her rhetoric intensified as the months progressed, but her chief adversary, New York's Archbishop Patrick Joseph Hayes, stood his ground and refused to back down from the fight. Hayes, who during World War I had been the first Catholic bishop of the U.S. armed forces and who would later be made a cardinal by Pope Pius XI, had a reputation as a strong leader. In December 1921, he issued a pastoral letter against birth control to be read at all the Masses throughout the diocese during Christmas time. He was drawing the battle lines and drawing them sharply. The *New York Times* quoted the letter at length:

> The Christ-Child did not stay His own entrance into this mortal life because his mother was poor, roofless, and without provision for the morrow. He knew that the Heavenly Father who cared for the lilies of the fields and the birds of the air loved the children of men more than

these. Children troop down from Heaven because God wills it. He alone has the right to stay their coming, while he blesses at will some homes with many, others with but a few or none at all. They come in the one way ordained by his wisdom. Woe to those who degrade, pervert, or do violence to the law of nature as fixed by the eternal decree of God Himself![1]

With the preaching of this letter throughout the diocese, there could be no question where Hayes and the Church stood on the issue of birth control. Like the bishops in 1919, he not only condemned the practice, but reaffirmed Church teaching on the necessity of obeying the fixed natural law, regardless of the circumstances. Birth control was evil, and man could never do something evil even for ostensibly good reasons. After this strong statement of divine law, Hayes's letter made an appeal to the heart:

Even though some little angels in the flesh, through the moral, mental or physical deformity of parents, may appear to human eyes hideous, misshapen, a blot on civilized society, we must not lose sight of this Christian thought that under and within such visible malformation there lives an immortal soul to be saved and glorified for all eternity among the blessed in heaven.[2]

With this last statement, Hayes was referring to the eugenic arguments Sanger and others were putting forward for birth control at this time. Using phrases such as "quality instead of quantity," they argued that high birth rates among the lower classes led to physically, mentally, and morally deformed children who would only go on to lives of misery and

[1]"Archbishop Hayes on Birth Control," *New York Times*, December 18, 1921, http://proquest.umi.com.ezproxy.mnsu.edu (accessed March 7, 2011).

[2]"Archbishop Hayes on Birth Control."

would continue to propagate their pathetic kind.[3] Hayes obviously did not accept this reasoning as a justification for birth control, and he urged his flock to reject it as well. In a clear reference to Sanger's work, he exhorted Catholic couples, "Stop your ears to that pagan philosophy . . . keep far from the sanctuary of your Christian homes, as you would an evil spirit, the literature of this unclean abomination."[4]

Sanger, of course, did not miss the opportunity to reply to Hayes and in so doing attempted yet again to rally non-Catholics to her side. In her reply, she once more professed a belief in American freedom of religion, even for Hayes, and contrasted that belief with the Catholic Church's alleged practice of suppressing opposing viewpoints. She furthermore restated her belief in a changeable moral code, shaped by the exigencies of the moment. "What [Hayes] believes concerning the soul after life," she said, "is based upon theory and he has a perfect right to that belief; but we, who are trying to better humanity fundamentally, believe that a healthy, happy human race is more in keeping with the laws of God than disease, misery and poverty perpetuating itself generation after generation." She continued:

> There is no objection to the Catholic Church inculcating the theories and doctrines in its own church and to its own people; but when they attempt to make these ideas

---

[3]This sort of reasoning found its way all the way up into the U.S. Supreme Court when in the 1927 case *Buck v. Bell*, Justice Oliver Wendell Holmes Jr. defended the forced sterilization of those society deemed unfit to procreate by infamously stating, "Three generations of imbeciles are enough." The only dissent in the case came from Justice Pierce Butler, a Catholic.

[4]"Archbishop Hayes on Birth Control." In another hard-hitting line from the letter, Hayes declared that "to take life after its inception is a horrible crime; but to prevent human life that the Creator is about to bring into being is satanic. In the first instance, the body is killed while the soul lives on: in the latter, not only the body but an immortal soul is denied existence in time and in eternity."

legislative acts and force their opinions and code of
morals upon the Protestant members of this country, then
we do consider this an interference with the principles of
this Democracy and we have a right to protest.[5]

Short of printing it in red, white, and blue type, Sanger
could not have made a statement appear more American. She
acknowledged American freedom of religion, even the freedom
for Catholics who opposed her to present their case. Whether
she actually believed Catholics should have this freedom is a
matter for debate, especially in light of later statements she
made, but she realized the use of such language helped connect
her birth control crusade with the cause of American freedom,
and that this resonated with the American people.[6] While
Sanger was thus engaged in associating birth control with liberty in the public mind, her *Birth Control Review* set out to
tear into Hayes and his pastoral letter. A February 1922 article
blasted the archbishop with the liberal use of such unflatter-
ingly descriptive words as "foolish," "absurd," and "asininity."
The writer declared that Hayes was "the incarnation of
Medievalism" and that "few have equaled him even in the
darkest ages of mankind." The article then directly attacked
Hayes's reference to the "little angels in the flesh," asking,

---

[5]Margaret Sanger, "Reply by Margaret Sanger to Archbishop Hayes'
Statement," (January 20 1922), in PWS,
http://www.nyu.edu/projects/sanger/webedition/app/documents/show.ph
p?sangerDoc=237427.xml (accessed December 14, 2010). Despite what
Sanger implied in her propaganda, the Catholic opposition was not trying to
make birth control illegal, but was trying to preserve the laws Protestants
had enacted against it.

[6]In 1957, Sanger appeared on *The Mike Wallace Interview*. Wallace
asked her if she believed Catholics had the right to argue against government
funding of birth control, since their tax dollars would go to pay for it. Sanger
said she believed they did, but Wallace then brought up the fact that the
show's reporter, having interviewed Sanger just a few days prior, quoted her
as saying it should be illegal for a church to forbid its members to practice
birth control. She flatly denied making the statement.

Are the children begotten in beastly passion by drunken fathers, and conceived by helpless, loathing mothers to be truthfully or even metaphorically described as little angels trooping down from heaven? It seems rather more fitting to think of them as little imps fished up from perdition. Surely, babes born of ignorance, and debauchery, of disease and crime . . . can not be regarded as having issued from Heaven, wherever Heaven is or whatever it may be. Would not the non-existence of such beings be better, all 'round, than their existence?[7]

The level of Sanger's association with the eugenics movement is still a topic of ardent debate, but it is evident from this article in her journal, and from statements she made, that she at least wished to reduce the number of "pauper children" and "idiots."[8] Archbishop Hayes stated that this in and of itself was not an unworthy goal, but that people could not use morally illicit means to reach it, and that it was better to accept potentially imperfect children rather than prevent their conception or birth by sinful means. Clearly, Sanger and her associates disagreed with Hayes, and they increasingly tried to show that the majority of Americans sided with them against the position of the Church. Sanger especially sought to emphasize, as time went on, that even Catholic women saw the necessity for birth control and frequented her clinics in large numbers. In this way, she worked to isolate the hierarchy and

---

[7]Ralcy Husted Bell, "In the Name of the Babe of Bethlehem," *Birth Control Review* 6, no. 2 (February 1922): 16–17, in *Birth Control Review* (New York: Da Capo Press, 1970).

[8]Esther Katz, an ardent defender of Sanger and editor of her papers, admits that "Sanger's adoption of eugenicist arguments, however progressive, led her to endorse some extremely problematic policies and to make some extremely unfortunate statements." At the same time, she laments that Sanger's words are often taken out of context and misinterpreted. See Esther Katz, "The Editor as Public Authority: Interpreting Margaret Sanger," *The Public Historian* 17, no. 1 (Winter 1995): 47.

those few Catholics they could "control," portraying them as the only opponents of birth control.

For Sanger, it was crucial to show that hers was a popular movement. Her opponents in the Church based many of their arguments on the natural law, which they said was written in the hearts of all men by God. If Sanger could show that the majority of people were in favor of birth control, she could more easily call the existence of this law into question in the public mind. As the guiding principle of her moral revolution against the idea of natural law and its corollary, fixed morality, Sanger argued that the American democratic tradition should be applied to the realm of morality. In this setting, every person's opinion was of equal value, and moral questions would be decided, like most questions in America, by the will of the majority. As she put it, "in the long run there is but one way to settle any question of morality, and that is by public opinion formed through honest discussion."[9] Such a view could not have been more opposed to Catholic teaching with its unchangeable moral order and strict hierarchical structure. Of the two positions, Sanger's sounded more thoroughly American, and she knew it. She increasingly portrayed the Catholic Church as a foreign element in America, dangerous to American liberties and intent on smothering freedom everywhere it could establish itself.

At times, Sanger's anti-Catholic rhetoric reached tones that almost seem laughable to a modern audience. Undoubtedly there were contemporary readers who thought the same, yet these early writings came in the wake of immensely popular and fanatically anti-Catholic publications such as *The Menace*. Sanger's sanctimonious use of "liberty-loving" language in a 1922 article entitled "Our Fight in New York" made it read more like a piece in *The Menace* than it did an article advocating a practice most American religious denominations still did not approve. In her appeal for Americans to protect

_____

[9]Margaret Sanger, "Church Control?" *Birth Control Review* 5, no. 12 (December 1921): 3–4, in *Birth Control Review* (New York: Da Capo Press, 1970), 17.

liberty by confronting the Church, Sanger exhibited an imagination worthy of history's best nativist writers as she called forth visions of the Church's dark, underhanded dealings throughout time, and of its attempts to secretly infiltrate all levels of society in order to hold people in ignorance:

I wish to call your attention to another brand of enemy, far more dangerous, more dastardly, more insidious. These are those who, from time immemorial, have been too tricky to fight in the open. Calumny, falsehood have been and are to-day their insidious weapons. Through the centuries these forces have attempted to check the progress of civilization. There is the underground root of fear and threat. They weave mysterious, intangible networks of influence. They place their intimidated henchmen in every sphere of public life.[10]

Sanger hoped the non-Catholic American mind would react as strongly to this description of the Church's mysterious, ethereal, and ever-present threat as it had in the past. Others in American history had successfully played the anti-Catholic card; she wished to do the same. She continued her vivid description of the Church's threat by once again proclaiming it the enemy of all that Americans revered, of which birth control was allegedly a logical extension. "The respectable elements of our national community," she said, "sit good-naturedly back, while these powers of darkness steadily spread their sphere of influence. Today they have centered their efforts on the Birth Control Movement. They have decided that they will crush out its life." She went on, explaining that these forces "realize that the splendid youthful vitality of this movement is a symbol of the growing power of science, human intelligence, enlightenment and liberty."

Science, intelligence, enlightenment, and liberty were

[10]Margaret Sanger, "Our Fight in New York," *Birth Control Review* (December 1922): 241, in PWS, http://www.nyu.edu/projects/sanger/webedition/app/documents/show.php?sangerDoc=229790.xml (accessed December 14, 2010).

of course, declared Sanger, the mortal enemies of a church that wished to maintain its medieval hold on the mind of man. "Crush [the birth control movement]," she said, "and the clock of human progress will be set back; human society will stagger through centuries of darkening obscurity into new dark ages, for upon the ruins of civilization, upon lies and deceit and ignorance these sinister influences flourish."[11]

With this last statement, Sanger dramatically raised the stakes. Earlier on, she told Americans they must accept birth control if they wished to avoid domination by the Catholic hierarchy, but now she claimed the entire life of the nation, of civilization itself, was endangered by Catholic opposition to her movement. Consequently, the fate of civilization was bound to the success of the birth control movement. If the movement failed, everything Americans knew would be lost as the world collapsed into a new dark age controlled by the Catholic Church. This was a rather dramatic scenario, but Sanger assured her readers that the threat to their freedom was very real indeed. She explained that the Catholic Church, through its puppet politicians, already had a stranglehold on American political life and was using it to enforce Catholic absolute morality in the United States. How could freedom-loving Americans accept this, she asked. The Church's control of American institutions threatened them as much as it did her. She described the necessity of resistance, saying,

> This is a matter of importance not merely to the Birth Control Movement in itself; it is of the gravest importance to the national life—to every true citizen of these United States. Are we to sit supinely back and witness without protest this insolent domination of American life and morals, by a small sect which has, for centuries, been inimical to the true interests of civilization and obstructive to the finer flowering of human genius? Are we to

---

[11]Sanger, "Our Fight in New York," 241.

permit these demagogues to batten on human misery, ignorance and stupidity?

Why, Sanger asked, did non-Catholics not defend their American liberties? Why did they not carry on the grand tradition of the American Revolution and resist domination by the Church? "The brave men and women who founded this Republic, did so to insure freedom of thought and religious opinion," she explained. "They sought primarily to avoid the domination of the political structure by any sect or creed, yet through fear, intimidation and a deplorable blindness to the spiritual values that lie at the foundation of liberty today, we have lost the courage to fight for this glorious heritage handed down to us by our noble forefathers."[12]

Like the Know-Nothings and American Protective Association before her, Sanger called on Americans not only to wake up to the shadowy-but-real threat the Church allegedly posed to their free way of life, but also to do something about the situation. It was their duty as Americans, she said, to carry on the struggle for liberty in the world. Just as they were exposing corruption in American business and politics during the Progressive Era, she charged they now had to do the same with their old enemy, the Church. It just so happened, she explained, that her birth control movement provided the perfect opportunity for Americans to once again stand up to this mysterious and ever-present threat. She described the situation:

Peculiarly, the Birth Control Movement seems to be active enough, strong enough and vital enough to bring this enemy out into the open. Now let us . . . expose the corrupt source of this sinister opposition. Let us unmask the enemy fearlessly and frankly and drive it out of the various avenues of our social and political structure, for no one can truly expect the benefits of freedom or liberty who is not willing to volunteer in this new and greater war of

---

[12]Sanger, "Our Fight in New York," 241.

defense, who is not willingly active and aggressively ready to defend our ancestral freedom against the dogmas of superstition.[13]

The Church was everywhere, Sanger warned, and in all places sought to subvert American liberties. Even in smaller communities, the Church threatened freedom through its requests for government funding of parochial schools.[14] To counteract these influences in even the remotest places of the country, Sanger instructed her readers to "ask an active personal investigation of the dominating religious and educational forces which are determining the political and social life and conditions in your own community." She finished her article by dramatically urging her readers to do their part in curbing clerical power. "Find out for yourself the source of the unsleeping opposition to the Birth Control Movement. Let us together watch, stand guardian at the gate of liberty!"[15]

---

[13]Sanger, "Our Fight in New York," 241.

[14]The issue of the schools, as nearly all historians of the Catholic Church in America relate, was highly contentious and caused a great deal of worry among non-Catholics. The demands of some prelates for public funding of parochial schools alarmed many Americans who decried it as a violation of the separation of church and state.

[15]Margaret Sanger, "Our Fight in New York,"241.

CHAPTER 5

THE NEW MORALITY

While Margaret Sanger's anti-Catholic propaganda and patriotic rhetoric could often reach melodramatic heights, she did at other times seek to draw public attention toward real Catholic efforts against her movement. The Catholic hierarchy and various Catholic organizations recognized Sanger's crusade for birth control as an attack on the traditional moral order and as time passed became ever more organized in their resistance efforts. Sanger in turn pointed to this increasingly systematized opposition as further proof that the Catholic Church was an outdated institution fighting desperately to maintain its moral control over humanity.

Perhaps more than any other Catholic organization, the Knights of Columbus proved to be a determined source of opposition to Sanger, just as they had to *The Menace* some years earlier. *The Menace* had often lampooned the Knights and their favorite method of coercion, the boycott, and Sanger now did the same.[1] She filled her writings with stories of rented meeting halls being withdrawn after their owners received Catholic boycott threats. At other times she recounted the

---

[1] See Justin Nordstrom's appendix in *Danger on the Doorstep: Anti-Catholicism and American Print Culture in the Progressive Era* (Notre Dame: University of Notre Dame Press, 2006).

bravery of hall owners who would not surrender to Catholic intimidation, but stood fast and allowed their establishments to be used for birth control meetings and lectures. A prime example of this was her retelling of events surrounding a birth control meeting in Cincinnati. She described how her "arch-enemies" sought to "hinder the progress of enlightenment" through the use of a Knights of Columbus boycott of the Hotel Gibson, which had agreed to host her conference. Sanger showered praise upon both the hotel and the city for their refusal to be intimidated out of giving her a forum. "To the everlasting credit of the managers of the hotel and the Mayor of Cincinnati," she said, "they stood firm." She continued:

> They upheld the law and the Constitution. They refused to be intimidated by this blustering mob, directed by the wily directors of Church politics. ... Let us not fail to record here our deep gratitude and appreciation for this noble support of the sacred American traditions of free speech and free thought. Cincinnati is to be congratulated for the fine courage and steadfastness of her mayor, her citizens, and the management of the Hotel Gibson, in resisting the threats of the Catholic machine.[2]

The American people, as Sanger saw it, were beginning to side with her on the issue of birth control, at least as far as her right to discuss it publicly. Opposition to birth control, as she described it, looked more and more like Catholic interference with American freedoms. Nevertheless, no major Protestant denomination had yet officially accepted birth control as a morally sound practice. Certainly there were individual religious leaders who approved of it, but no significant religious body officially allowed its use. Sanger believed, or at least claimed to believe, that fear of the Catholic Church kept Protestants from condoning birth control. Writing later of a

---

[2]Margaret Sanger, "Facing the New Year," *Birth Control Review* (January 1923): 3–4, in PWS, http://www.nyu.edu/projects/sanger/webedition/app/documents/show.php?sangerDoc=210661.xml (accessed December 14, 2010).

reserved statement by an English Quaker committee which had acknowledged that birth control methods other than abstinence might be acceptable, Sanger goaded American Protestant denominations, saying, "The Society of Friends is brave enough, as all other Protestant bodies should be, to announce publicly its independence from the domination of the Roman Catholic Church in this all-important problem, in that it refuses to rule out the discussion and the spread of knowledge concerning Birth Control."[3] American Protestant denominations, proclaimed Sanger, had just as much responsibility to declare their freedom from the Catholic Church as individual American citizens did.

It is doubtful whether Protestants demurred on the issue of birth control out of a fear of the Catholic Church. It seems more likely they were still uncomfortable with Sanger's talk of the moral revolution intrinsically present in the acceptance of birth control. In a 1929 article entitled "The Civilizing Force of Birth Control," Sanger made it clear that she was indeed fighting to overturn the old, absolute moral order associated with the Catholic Church, and that she wished thereby to usher in a new civilization based upon a new, pragmatic morality. She began by complaining that "because of its misuse and abuse by reactionaries and defenders of the status quo, the term 'morality' has come to connote . . . practically everything that is distasteful to the spirit of progress." She pointed to the Catholic Church's monopoly on the idea of morality as the reason for this backwardness:

The authority on which this opposition of the Roman Catholic Church against birth control is based is the conception that there is only one true Church, and subsequently only one true morality. It is claimed that the Catholic Church is the depository of eternal truth, the

---

[3]Margaret Sanger, "One Week's Activity in England," *Birth Control Review* (August 1925): 219–20, in PWS, http://www.nyu.edu/projects/sanger/webedition/app/documents/show.php?sangerDoc=205948.xml (accessed December 14, 2010).

Kingdom of God on earth. The Catholic Church ... is therefore responsible for the morals of the entire human race. It is the duty of the Church, therefore, to interfere with and to block all legislation that may adversely affect the "morals" of non-Catholics as well as Catholics.[4]

Sanger went on to complain in rather strong language that the Catholic Church's "closed" moral system was oppressive of personal liberty as it would not allow individuals to make their own choices in matters of sexual morality. The Catholic Church, she stated, was guilty of moral oppression, and every denomination that insisted on an absolute moral code was complicit in the Church's tyranny. She wrote:

This Catholic system of morality is the archetype of all ethical systems which rest upon unquestioning obedience of higher authorities. ... Conformity, respect for all external laws, and a blind and bland indifference to anything except the preordained and predetermined 'plan of God' as formulated by the accented authorities, are the essential virtues accentuated by all such closed systems of morality.[5]

Fortunately, said Sanger, the world in the centuries since the Enlightenment had been turning more and more against the dictatorship of the Church and its fixed morality. She explained that people were gradually looking away from God for moral guidance and instead making moral decisions for themselves. They were embracing the new, pragmatic morality as they discarded the old moral system. Sanger praised this moral progressivism as she wrote,

---

[4]Margaret Sanger, "The Civilizing Force of Birth Control," 1929, in Calverton and S.D. Schmalhausen, eds., *Sex in Civilization* (Garden City, NY: 1939), 525–537, in PWS, http://www.nyu.edu/projects/sanger/webedition/app/documents/show.php?sangerDoc=320525.xml (accessed December 14, 2010).

[5]Sanger, "The Civilizing Force of Birth Control."

Against such "morality," the spirit of Western Civilization is revolting with ever-increasing vigor. There has been a revolution in the world of morality of which we are now beginning to taste the first fruits. We are no longer living in a little closed completed universe of which God's plan was revealed once and for all time to a little group of delegates. The center of our universe has shifted from Heaven to earth.[6]

Sanger went on to say that the moral revolution owed much to the Church's supposed natural enemies, philosophy and science, which had "destroyed the old concept of the absolute." Because of this progress, humanity no longer relied on an absolute moral system, but was free to discover its own morality by trial and error. The new moral system, Sanger claimed, not only supplanted the old system, but turned that system upside down. "The revealed and dogmatic basis of morality, as expressed by the Roman Catholics, and as accepted by so many other unthinking religious organizations," she said, "has lost its old authority. Where the dogmatists read black, the world to-day is reading white. What they consider 'morality' we consider moral imbecility ... our morality is ... a morality of reality, aiming to show men and women the structure of their relationships to each other, to the world at large, and the world to be." Birth control, she concluded, would be, "a power for the development of the new morality."[7]

In addition to promoting this new moral code, Sanger hoped to see the creation of a new civilization based upon it. She explained her desire to fashion a new society rooted in the superior morality of experience. She argued this was the correct form of true civilization, one in which morality was discovered by trial and error and decided upon by the people. She saw the acceptance of birth control as a fundamental principle of this new, liberated civilization, and she explained that this

---

[6]Sanger, "The Civilizing Force of Birth Control."

[7]Sanger, "The Civilizing Force of Birth Control."

acceptance "by ever increasing numbers of intelligent and prudent people in all civilized countries" was proof that the development of this new society was underway. That the acceptance of birth control was still limited in western society she blamed on the fact that "Occidental folkways have been based upon an outgrown medieval theology which even day-to-day exerts an incalculably dysgenic influence upon the race." Her fight, in essence, was not just for birth control. It was a campaign to build a new civilization free of absolute morality. It was a crusade, as she put it, "to effect humanity's liberation from the destructive slave-morality promulgated for so many centuries past."[8]

---

[8]Sanger, "The Civilizing Force of Birth Control."

CHAPTER 6

VICTORIES FOR BIRTH CONTROL

Margaret Sanger firmly believed that the acceptance of birth control entailed a moral revolution. As she saw it, traditional moral taboos had too long repressed the world. Above all else, she blamed the Catholic Church for maintaining and enforcing these moral ideals even into the twentieth century. It is possible that at least some of the more conservative and moderate Protestant denominations feared Sanger's absolute rejection of objective morality even more than they feared Catholic encroachments on American freedoms. Sanger's radicalism undoubtedly made them cautious about her birth control crusade, but within a short time they would embrace her cause. This shift began most prominently with the Anglican Lambeth Conference of 1930.

At the 1930 Lambeth Conference, the Anglican Church became the first mainstream Protestant denomination to officially move from condemnation of birth control to acceptance of birth control, though it did so with significant reservation.[1]

---

[1]Kathleen Tobin shows that some of the more liberal denominations, including the Unitarians and Universalists as well as some Methodists, made their own permissive statements on the use of birth control shortly before Lambeth 1930. See Tobin-Schelsinger, "Population and Power," 212–22.

At its 1920 conference, it had forbidden the practice in fairly certain terms, but at Lambeth 1930, it declared that the use of birth control was permissible if done for serious reasons:

> Where there is clearly felt moral obligation to limit or avoid parenthood, the method must be decided on Christian principles. . . . [I]n those cases where there is such a clearly felt moral obligation to limit or avoid parenthood, and where there is a morally sound reason for avoiding complete abstinence, the Conference agrees that other methods may be used, provided that this is done in the light of the same Christian principles. The Conference records its strong condemnation of the use of any methods of conception control from motives of selfishness, luxury, or mere convenience.[2]

While very reserved by modern standards and in no way endorsing the unrestricted use of birth control, Lambeth 1930 is often viewed as a watershed moment in the official acceptance of birth control by Protestants, as other denominations throughout the world gradually felt emboldened to follow up with permissive statements of their own.[3] That Sanger herself was immensely pleased with the Lambeth statement is revealed in her personal correspondence.[4] It seemed to her that religious bodies were finally opening up to her movement, but as the Anglican Church was cracking its door for the accep-

---

Tobin also explains that the Lambeth Conference did not immediately set off a great wave of permissive statements from Protestant groups, but that many Protestants, especially the more conservative, still had significant reservations, even in the years following the conference. However, she does admit that the conference "marked a profound change in official religious teaching regarding birth control that would influence other denominations as well." See Kathleen A. Tobin, *The American Religious Debate Over Birth Control, 1907–1937* (Jefferson, NC: McFarland and Company, 2001), 51–52.

[2]Lambeth Conference 1930, Resolution 15, "The Life and Witness of the Christian Community – Marriage and Sex," http://www.lambethconference.org/resolutions/1930/1930–15.cfm (accessed March 7, 2011).

tance of birth control, the pope in Rome was bracing that door shut for Catholics.

In December 1930, Pope Pius XI issued his encyclical *Casti Connubii* or "Of Chaste Marriage." That it came on the heels of the 1930 Lambeth Conference was not a coincidence. In the encyclical, the pope strongly condemned divorce, eugenics, abortion, and, of course, birth control. He strongly reaffirmed the principles of natural law and the Church's role in preserving morality for all men. While the pope did not aim the encyclical at Sanger specifically, he could just as well have, as it directly attacked the idea of a new morality founded on science, experience, and consensus. As Sanger read the encyclical, she must have felt the pope was referring to her as he warned of "the false principles of a new and utterly perverse morality." Later in the same letter, he struck at the heart of her appeal for a new scientific moral system as he explained,

> Books are not lacking which dare to pronounce them-
> selves as scientific but which in truth are merely coated
> with a veneer of science in order that they may the more
> easily insinuate their ideas. The doctrines defended in

---

[3]Richard Fagley relates that in March 1931, the U.S. Federal Council of Churches' Committee on Marriage and Home declared, "the careful and restrained use of contraceptives by married people is valid and moral." See Richard M. Fagley, *The Population Explosion and Christian Responsibility* (New York: Oxford University Press, 1960). Allen Carlson, in his work *Godly Seed*, explains that several member churches of the Federal Council of Churches strongly protested the birth control statement, with some even leaving or threatening to leave over the issue. Despite outward appearances, many Protestant denominations still vehemently opposed the use of birth control. Sanger, meanwhile, began giving secret donations to the Federal Council of Churches in order to support its developing pro-birth-control stance. See Allan Carlson, *Godly Seed: American Evangelicals Confront Birth Control, 1873–1973* (New Brunswick, NJ: Transaction Publishers, 2012), 104–5.

[4]Sanger to Abby Aldrich Rockefeller, September 29, 1930, in Esther Katz, ed., *The Selected Papers of Margaret Sanger, Volume 2: Birth Control Comes of Age, 1928–1939* (Chicago: University of Illinois Press, 2006), 77.

these are offered for sale as the productions of modern genius, of that genius namely, which, anxious only for truth, is considered to have *emancipated* itself from all those old-fashioned and immature opinions of the ancients; and to the number of these antiquated opinions they relegate the traditional doctrine of Christian marriage.[5]

At the core of the pope's encyclical was the doctrine of absolute and unchangeable natural law. Scientific experimentation, philosophical reasoning, and group consensus, the pope declared, could not make something moral if God himself had declared it immoral. Not even the Church could do this. Based on this doctrine, the pope explained that the use of artificial means of birth control could never be justified. "But no reason, however grave," he said, "may be put forward by which anything intrinsically against nature may become conformable to nature and morally good." He further explained, "Since, therefore, the conjugal act is destined primarily by nature for the begetting of children, those who in exercising it deliberately frustrate its natural power and purpose sin against nature and commit a deed which is shameful and intrinsically vicious."[6]

With his encyclical, the pope drew a sharp line in the sand. Whereas Sanger argued that the world needed to accept birth control and embrace a new morality based on science and distinct from any God-given law, the pope proclaimed that birth control needed to be condemned because it was a violation of the unchangeable natural law laid down by God himself. Furthermore, he reaffirmed the Church's duty to safeguard the moral order for all people, Catholic and non-Catholic alike. In a resounding statement of papal authority,

5Pius XI, *Casti Connubii*, December 1930, Vatican: The Holy See, inhttp://www.vatican.va/holy_father/pius_xi/encyclicals/documents/hf_p-xi_enc_31121930_casti-connubii_en.html. (accessed January 17, 2011).

6Pius XI, *Casti Connubii*.

of the role of the Church as the guardian of morality, and of the evil of birth control, the pope declared,

> Since, therefore, openly departing from the uninterrupted Christian tradition some recently have judged it possible solemnly to declare another doctrine regarding this question, the Catholic Church, to whom God has entrusted the defense of the integrity and purity of morals, standing erect in the midst of the moral ruin which surrounds her, in order that she may preserve the chastity of the nuptial union from being defiled by this foul stain, raises her voice in token of her divine ambassadorship and through Our mouth proclaims anew: any use whatsoever of matrimony exercised in such a way that the act is deliberately frustrated in its natural power to generate life is an offense against the law of God and of nature, and those who indulge in such are branded with the guilt of a grave sin.[7]

The pope's reference to those who "have judged it possible solemnly to declare another doctrine" was aimed at the Anglican bishops, but Sanger understandably felt targeted by the encyclical as well. She quickly penned a response in which she reaffirmed her belief in the necessity of using science and experience in determining morality. She explained how the pope's encyclical "aims to regulate the conjugal affairs of Catholic men and women, without the benefit of science, and according to theories written by St. Augustine, also a bachelor, who died fifteen centuries ago." She went on, saying, "The Pope makes it perfectly plain that Catholics are expected to give up health, happiness, and life itself while making every other conceivable sacrifice rather than to have dominion over nature's processes of procreation."[8]

---

[7]Pius XI, *Casti Connubii.*

[8]Margaret Sanger, "Birth Control Advances: A Reply to the Pope," 1931, in PWS, http://www.nyu.edu/projects/sanger/webedition/app/documents/show.php?sangerDoc=236637.xml (accessed December 14, 2010).

Sanger understood the pope's message as a concrete challenge to her pragmatic moral philosophy. She recognized in his statements on natural law a direct attack on the new morality and her new civilization, and she probably realized the pope's actions would fortify Catholic opposition to birth control, making her work among Catholics more difficult. At the same time, she tried to use the pope's declaration to her advantage, quoting it as further proof that the Catholic Church was outdated and had no respect for American liberties. She even claimed the birth control movement should be flattered and encouraged by the pope's statement, explaining her belief that he had chosen this time to issue it because he was "alarmed" at the progress of the movement. She elaborated, saying the pope "admits that a new and, as he thinks, 'utterly perverse' morality is 'gradually gaining ground.' . . . We need not wonder what he means. He makes specific and repeated references to birth control by contraceptive measures as a main object of his attack." In yet another effort to portray her cause as thoroughly American, she then mentioned "in passing" that the pope claimed to be the "only authorized guardian and interpreter of a 'Divine law' applying to marriage." She contrasted this with her own position on religion, saying, "I believe people have a right to worship in their own way, providing they do not impose their doctrines upon me."[9]

After contrasting the democratic spirit of her movement with the pope's paternal claim to religious and moral authority, Sanger expressed her satisfaction that other churches were updating their positions on birth control after their own periods of resistance to it. She especially commended the Anglican bishops, but also gave a long list of the other "converts to scientific control."[10] In contrast to the progressive stance these numerous other religious bodies were taking on birth control, Sanger bleakly described the situation in Rome. "The world moves, but the Pope sits still. He declares that he is 'looking with paternal eye . . . as from a watch-tower.'

9Sanger, "Birth Control Advances."

But what is he looking at? Mostly old books, the musty writings of ancient busy-bodies who took a neurotic delight in telling folks what they must not do, arguing theories characteristic of the Dark Ages." She went on, pressing her accusation that the Catholic hierarchy clung to an outdated moral system. "The pope," she said, "refuses to abandon the ancient and moth-eaten arguments of the Catholic Church against the limitation of offspring." Finally, she accused him of being oblivious to the suffering in the world outside the Vatican, or of even enjoying people's pain. "I want to say that his attitude in general is characterized by disapproval of human enjoyment and an apparent relishing of the theory that suffering is good for our souls."[11]

For Sanger, the Catholic Church's refusal to embrace the new morality was evidence of its scientific backwardness and lust for control through ignorance. In her commentary on

---

[10]Sanger's list of "other religious and social groups that have expressed themselves, with more or less reservation, as sanctioning scientific birth control" included the Conference of Congregational Churches of Connecticut; the Conference of Methodist Episcopal Churches (New York East); the 55th Southern California Conference of the Methodist Episcopal Church; the Universalist General Convention; the American Unitarian Association; the Community Church, New York; the Central Conference of American Rabbis (Baltimore); the Legislative Committee of the Ethical Culture Society; the City Federation of Women's Clubs, New York; the League of Women Voters, New York City; the New York League of Women Workers; the Junior League of New York; the New Jersey Women's Republican Club; and the Legislative Committee of the Federation for Child Study. By contrast, in 1931, the evangelical magazine *Moody Bible Institute Monthly* published an editorial lauding Pius XI and his encyclical, while at the same time expressing a desire that Protestant denominations would find the courage to speak out as boldly. See Allan Carlson, *Godly Seed: American Evangelicals Confront Birth Control, 1873–1973* (New Brunswick, NJ: Transaction Publishers, 2012), 107–8.

[11]Sanger, "Birth Control Advances."

Casti Connubii, she connected the Church with a "Dark Ages" opposition to scientific advancement and with hostility toward the principles of American freedom. She lamented that the Church would not bring its moral code up to date, but she took consolation in her belief that other churches were embracing the new morality. Fortunately, she said, despite the Catholic Church's opposition, the increasing acceptance of birth control by other religious and social organizations was "a feature of a new civilization which is gradually escaping the clutches of ignorance, superstition and tyranny."[12]

Sanger made every effort to turn the pope's encyclical into propaganda for her campaign. Her dramatic language and witty remarks, however, did not fully express the deep-seated loathing she had for the Church. This was more clearly shown in her personal correspondence. For example, in a letter to British sexologist Havelock Ellis, Sanger professed her happiness with the Spanish Republican government's persecution of Catholics. She explained to Ellis, "Spain to me is gloriously vindicating my love of her these days burning down convents & Smoking out the religious enemies."[13] A few years later, she suggested in another letter that the United States might have its own persecution of the Church. She wrote of efforts by Catholics against her movement and explained that "people are so indignant all over the country over their arrogant interference that it would not take much to turn that indignation into an anti-Catholic uprising. In fact, it is bound to come some day if they keep on minding other people's business and imposing their religious stupidity upon the rest of us."[14]

These statements reveal that Sanger's anti-Catholic propaganda was more than a rhetorical act. She genuinely saw

---

[12]Sanger, "Birth Control Advances."

[13]Sanger to Havelock Ellis, November 28, 1931, in Katz, *The Selected Papers, Volume 2,* 117.

[14]Sanger to Edith How-Martyn, February 1, 1934, in Katz, *The Selected Papers, Volume 2,* 269.

the Church as her arch-enemy and as the greatest obstacle to her new morality. After *Casti Connubii*, she continued her use of patriotic and anti-Catholic rhetoric, increasingly portraying herself as a kind of whistleblower, alerting the American people to the way the Catholic Church was using its power to interfere with the birth control movement. In a 1932 newsletter, she recounted her campaigns in various U.S. cities and described the opposition the Church gave her in each one. "My recent experiences, while on a speaking tour, have shown me the extent to which the Roman Catholic Church dictates the policy of the municipal authorities in many of our cities."[15] Most of the stories she told were essentially the same. She recounted how time and again, open-minded people invited her to speak, but the Church tried to stop her by using underhanded means, including threats of boycotts and pressure on public officials. The stories often ended happily for her followers, as enlightened citizens of the cities defended her and found a way around the manipulations of the Church, thus allowing her to speak to the great numbers who came eager for information and public discourse on birth control. She especially emphasized that public outcry against the machinations of the Church could often result in a victory for birth control. In this way, she continued encouraging people to stand up to the Church on birth control as a matter of American freedom.

Even while Sanger celebrated the popular support she increasingly received in the nation, she decried the double standard she saw in the government's continued enforcement of remaining anti-birth-control laws. She complained that in New Haven she was not allowed to speak in favor of birth control at a junior high school, but the following week a Catholic priest was able to speak against birth control at a similar meeting in the city. "One can see," she said, "that in the State of Connecticut, it is legal and moral to speak *against* a subject, but it seems unlawful to speak for the same subject; in other

---

[15]Margaret Sanger, "News Letter From Mrs. Sanger," 1932, in PWS, http://www.nyu.edu/projects/sanger/webedition/app/documents/ show.php?sangerDoc=130871.xml (accessed December 14, 2010).

words, freedom of speech depends upon which side you are on."[16] This double standard, Sanger believed, became even sharper with the publication in 1932 of Dr. Leo Latz's *The Rhythm of Sterility and Fertility in Women.* In *The Rhythm,* Latz, a Catholic medical doctor, offered an alternative to artificial means of birth control with what became known as the "rhythm method." The book claimed to be published with the approval of American Catholic authorities, and the Post Office apparently did not consider it banned from distribution under the Comstock Act, a fact which Sanger made sure to point out.[17]

Sanger offered a mixed reaction to *The Rhythm.* Privately, she wrote that it was "amazing," and she explained, "I'm reading it carefully . . . really it's significant."[18] She even publicly praised Latz's work insofar as it acknowledged there were circumstances in which it was permissible to avoid conception, but she complained the method he advocated was not effective. Even while she admired his "fearless intelligence and spirit that one respects," she openly wondered why the Post Office allowed his book through the mail when it did not

---

[16]Sanger, "News Letter From Mrs. Sanger."

[17]See Leo J. Latz, *The Rhythm of Sterility and Fertility in Women: A discussion of the physiological, practical, and ethical aspects of the discoveries of Drs. K. Ogino (Japan) and H. Knaus (Austria) regarding the periods when conception is impossible and when possible* (Chicago: Latz Foundation, 1958). The publication of *The Rhythm* caused significant debate within the Catholic Church and even resulted in Latz losing his position at Loyola University Medical School. As his 1994 obituary in the *Chicago Tribune* explains, "Cardinal George Mundelein, then archbishop of Chicago, approved the pamphlet, but later withdrew his blessing." See Kenan Heise, "Dr. Leo Latz, 91," *Chicago Tribune,* May 4, 1994, http://articles.chicagotribune.com/1994-05-04/news/9405040253_1_28-day-menstrual-cycle-loyola-university-medical-school-birth-control (accessed December 16, 2013).

[18]Sanger to Juliet Barrett Rublee, January 9, 1933, in Katz, *The Selected Papers, Volume 2,* 209.

permit works advocating other means of birth control to pass. "The federal laws," she observed, "state clearly that *'any'* information to prevent conception, sent through the United States Mails is illegal. The Post Office has informed us that 'Rhythm' by Dr. Latz is mailable, but that 'Contraceptive Practices' by Dr. Hannah M. Stone, is unmailable."[19] Why was a government agency showing preference for a method of birth control accepted by Catholics, she asked. "The twenty million members of the Catholic Faith now have a method of Birth Control legally sanctioned by the Post Office authorities and morally sanctioned by the hierarchy," she said. "But what about the one hundred and four millions of non-Catholics who prefer *other* methods of birth control?"[20]

Even while Sanger complained of the Post Office's uneven treatment of birth control information, the case that would grant her a great moral victory was making its way through the legal system. It originated in 1932 when U.S. Customs confiscated a shipment of birth control devices en route to Sanger from Japan. Sanger and her allies saw a chance to challenge the Federal Comstock laws, and after a series of legal maneuvers, they succeeded in bringing the case before the courts. In 1936, the United States Court of Appeals of the Second District issued its ruling in *United States v. One Package of Japanese Pessaries*. In that ruling, the court declared the Comstock Act could not be used to prevent physicians from importing birth control materials.[21] Sanger excit-

---

[19]Margaret Sanger, "Catholics and Birth Control," *New Republic* 79, no. 1019 (June 13, 1934): 129, in PWS, http://www.nyu.edu /projects/sanger/webedition/app/documents/show.php?sanger Doc=158 426.xml (accessed December 14, 2010).

[20]Sanger, "Catholics and Birth Control."

[21]Technically, the case addressed the 1930 Tariff Act, which applied the guidelines of the Comstock Act to imports. The court, in an effort to make birth control laws consistent, referred to previous rulings which allowed physicians to receive contraceptives through the mail if they were prescribing them to patients for medical reasons.

edly described the outcome in a private letter. "We won!!," she wrote. "This is a genuine victory & now if this opinion holds we are free from the drudgery of Federal work!! again good news! Thank God for this victory."[22]

Her success in the *One Package* case, along with previous smaller victories in similar cases, allowed Sanger to report publicly in a more measured tone that the birth control movement was making definite progress in the United States. In a 1937 article entitled "At Long Last," she celebrated the achievements of the movement thus far. She explained that at the beginning "fears and taboos, inertia and bigotry, ignorance and dogma blocked the path," but that "one by one these barriers have been cleared away." She continued, "Support from individual physicians with vision and courage came first. Support from leading religious denominations soon followed." She then explained,

> Even the Catholic Church, previously the outstanding enemy of birth control, was forced to recognize the need for family limitation when it sponsored the rhythm, or so-called safe period, method. Dr. Leo Latz's book, The Rhythm, which carries on its fly-leaf the phrase "Published With Ecclesiastical Approbation," gives reasons for family limitation which agree point for point with those advocated in birth-control literature. The Catholic Church has wriggled out of its absurd and inconsistent position by conceding the truth of the principles of birth control, but it differs on methods.[23]

---

[22]Sanger to Edith How-Martyn, December 12, 1936, in Katz, *The Selected Papers, Volume 2*, 386.

[23]Margaret Sanger, "At Long Last," *New Masses* (July 6, 1937): 19–20, in PWS, http://www.nyu.edu/projects/sanger/webedition/app/documents/show.php?sangerDoc=224215.xml (accessed December 16, 2013). It should be noted here that back during the 1921 Town Hall controversy, Archbishop Patrick Hayes had stated that some of the goals of birth control advocates were of themselves worthy, but that it was not permissible to use evil means to reach them.

While Sanger's celebratory statement made it seem her victory was won, she was sure to emphasize that the movement still had a long way to go. At the same time, while she praised the apparently liberalizing step of the Catholic Church in ostensibly approving the rhythm method, she stressed else-where that she strongly disagreed with the Church on the method's effectiveness. In a private letter to Herbert R. Mayes, editor of the woman's magazine *Pictorial Review*, she casti-gated him for the publication's advocacy of *The Rhythm*. She wrote, "I can quite appreciate that the *Pictorial Review* has a better chance to get through the Post Office censorship by advocating this Roman Catholic theory, but I can only say 'Shame upon you for doing so.'"[24] In addition, she continued worrying that Catholics would seek to overturn the *One Package* ruling or otherwise attempt to restrict access to birth control. She still saw the Church as her enemy and hoped to keep public opinion against it. In a letter to Rev. George Winslow Plummer, founder and Supreme Magus of the occult *Societas Rosicruciana* in America, she emphasized the need for continued cooperation against the Church by non-Catholic Americans. "We have all finally come to the decision that 'in union there is strength' and we need that strength to combat the devilish propaganda of the Roman Catholic Church."[25]

The 1930s saw a number of important victories for Margaret Sanger and the birth control movement. Success in the courts loosened government prohibitions against birth control, and favorable declarations by various religious groups

---

[24]Sanger to Herbert R. Mayes, April 11, 1938, in Katz, *The Selected Papers, Volume 2*, 441.

[25]Sanger to Rev. George Winslow Plummer, February 5, 1939, in Katz, *The Selected Papers, Volume 2*, 484. Sanger was herself a member of the Rosicrucians, a fact which could only have further increased the ani-mosity between her and the Church, given the popes' numerous condemna-tions of secret societies. See Ellen Chesler, *Woman of Valor: Margaret Sanger and the Birth Control Movement in America* (New York, Simon & Schuster, 1992), 135–36.

greatly lessened opposition to the practice of birth control among many of the official churches, with the obvious exception of the Catholic Church. At the same time, Sanger had made it clear that the birth control revolution was a moral revolution against the old, absolute moral code represented by the Catholic Church. Pope Pius XI's encyclical letter *Casti Connubii* made it just as clear that the Church would continue to vehemently oppose artificial means of birth control and reject both Sanger's new morality and the new civilization she hoped to found upon it.

For Sanger, the pope's encyclical provided further ammunition for the propaganda campaign she was waging against the Church in America. Early in her crusade, she had portrayed the fight for birth control as a fight for American freedom against the tyranny and backwardness of the Church. This propaganda, which dramatically escalated in 1921 after the police raid on her New York Town Hall meeting, continued at least until her 1936 victory in *One Package*. Despite winning that case, Sanger maintained her distrust of the Catholic Church and rightly feared continued campaigns against birth control by American Catholic organizations. She had ably exploited the 1921 Town Hall incident and the 1930 papal encyclical to portray opposition to birth control as Catholic opposition to science and American freedom. Now other people and events in the post-World War II era through the 1960s would help solidify this image.

CHAPTER 7

SANGER'S RHETORIC GOES MAINSTREAM

From the 1940s through the 1960s, the new morality and new civilization championed by Margaret Sanger took shape in the United States. Official Catholic opposition to these ideas remained in the hierarchy's continued condemnations of birth control, which in turn led to the solidification of the idea that opposition to it was solely a Catholic affair. During this time, Sanger's arguments that Catholic hostility to birth control was indicative of a broader disdain for science and American liberty became mainstream, largely through the efforts of her friend and fellow leftist radical, Paul Blanshard. By the end of the 1960s, a definite battle line on birth control had been drawn between proponents of the new morality and the Catholic Church. Prominent spokespersons defined this line through a series of important events in the decades following the Second World War.

In the early 1940s, the United States found itself fighting alongside the Allied Powers in World War II. As in the First World War, American Catholics saw the conflict as an opportunity to show their patriotism and commitment to the American ideal of freedom. Still, they suffered a persistent scrutiny of their Church, including comparisons of it to America's fascist enemies. Even while the war focused the nation's attention on external foes, some non-Catholic Americans concerned themselves with alleged similarities between the rigid belief system of the Catholic Church and the totalitarian authority exercised by the Axis regimes. They attacked the Church for being undemocratic and dogmatic in much the same way Sanger described it in her birth control campaigns.[1]

With the end of the war in 1945, the large number of returning GIs caused great changes in the social structure of the United States. Soldiers, who had spent the last few years interacting with and fighting alongside other soldiers of different creeds, had learned firsthand that they had more in common with their fellow Americans than they had previously believed. On their return home, many of them took advantage of the GI Bill and pursued a post-secondary education. For most Catholics, this was a new opportunity. Before the war, the majority of Catholics had belonged to the working class, but with this new access to higher education, they began achieving upward social mobility. With this rising social status, many younger Catholics began moving out of ethnic city neighborhoods and into the suburbs where they had even greater interaction with Americans of other religious traditions, thereby weakening the image of the Catholic Church as an entirely foreign element in America.

While it may have seemed that Catholics were becoming more like their non-Catholic neighbors in the years following the end of World War II, a number of issues still caused some friction between the Catholic Church and non-Catholic American society. Foremost among these was the issue of birth control. A 1948 referendum in Massachusetts to liberalize the state's strict anti-birth-control laws showed the extent to which the Church could go in its efforts to keep birth control illegal. The Massachusetts Catholic hierarchy and clergy waged a highly organized campaign to turn out the Catholic vote and defeat the bill. Their successful effort gave

---

[1]John T. McGreevy, *Catholicism and American Freedom: A History* (New York: W.W. Norton, 2003), 177–80; Jay P. Dolan, *In Search of an American Catholicism: A History of Religion and Culture in Tension* (New York: Oxford University Press, 2002), 164–65.

many the impression that Sanger was not far off in her dire warnings about the Catholic hierarchy manipulating the political system against birth control.[2] The following year, Sanger's good friend Paul Blanshard became a best-selling author and the century's most renowned critic of Catholic political influence in America with his highly acclaimed book, *American Freedom and Catholic Power*.

Paul Blanshard was a graduate of Harvard Divinity School who early on abandoned the tenets of Christianity and became an atheist and a staunch socialist. It was during his time as a preacher at the radical Maverick Church in East Boston that he first met and befriended Sanger.[3] While Blanshard never had any great affection for the Catholic Church, he explained in *American Freedom and Catholic Power* that it was the issue of birth control that drew him to his mission of exposing the Church's imminent threat to American liberties. He explained how he had experienced a growing concern about the world population problem, and how he "had come to feel that organized clerical fanaticism was the most serious obstacle to constructive remedies in this field." He associated this "clerical fanaticism" with the Catholic Church as he explained that "Although the Catholic Church did not play an important part in the opposition to birth control in the United States before 1914, it took the lead against Margaret Sanger as soon as she had launched a formal birth-control movement." He complained of Catholic boycotts against birth control supporters and declared that with Pius XI's promulgation of *Casti*

---

[2]Leslie Woodcock Tentler, *Catholics and Contraception: An American History* (Ithaca, NY: Cornell University Press, 2004), 170. During this campaign, the Catholic faction showed that it would not be outdone in the use of strong propaganda. One particularly graphic piece showed a knife-wielding hand representing the birth control movement. The hand prepared to plunge a dagger into a sleeping baby meant to symbolize the children of the future.

[3]Paul Blanshard, *Personal and Controversial: An Autobiography by Paul Blanshard* (Boston: Beacon Press, 1973), 33.

Connubii, "the hierarchy became the world's contraceptive enemy No. 1."[4]

While Blanshard's work sought to expose the Catholic threat to American freedom in many different areas, the prominence he gave to its opposition to birth control helped solidify the Church's reputation in that regard. The book's huge popularity, boosted by enthusiastic reviews from such prominent figures as John Dewey, Bertrand Russell, and Albert Einstein, ensured the wide dissemination of the theory that Catholic hostility to birth control sprang from an innate scientific backwardness and aversion to American freedom.[5]

Blanshard's explanation that it was the fear of overpopulation which drew him to birth control and to his denunciations of the Church demonstrates his belief in the new, pragmatic morality. Birth control was morally right, he believed, because it was necessary for combatting population growth. This was not a new idea. Concerns about the growing world population had existed since the preceding century and in the twentieth century became linked with arguments for birth control.[6] Sanger's *Birth Control Review* had dedicated a number of articles to the topic, using such titles as "Contraception Necessary and Therefore Moral."[7] Like Sanger, Blanshard repeatedly decried what he saw as the medieval and unscien-

---

[4]Paul Blanshard, *American Freedom and Catholic Power* (Boston: Beacon Press, 1949), 138.

[5]McGreevy, *Catholicism and American Freedom*, 166–68.

[6]The works of British Rev. Thomas Malthus (1766–1834) first brought attention to the possible population problem. Early twentieth-century population control advocates commonly became known as neo-Malthusians, even though Malthus himself preferred non-artificial means of birth control, such as delayed marriage.

[7]B. Dunlop, "Contraception Necessary and Therefore Moral" *Birth Control Review* 8, no. 5 (May 1924): 146–147, in *Birth Control Review* (New York: Da Capo Press, 1970).

tific attitude of the Church on birth control and contrasted it with the "realism" embraced by birth control's supporters.[8]

American Freedom and Catholic Power made Blanshard a sort of expert on Catholicism in Protestant eyes. His prominent affiliation with the watchdog group Protestants and Other Americans United for the Separation of Church and State (POAU) further strengthened this image. While many Protestant churches accepted birth control in the years immediately following the 1930 Lambeth Conference declaration, conservative Protestant groups continued the debate on birth control's morality at least through the 1950s. Blanshard played a role in this debate, despite the great ideological divide between him and conservative Protestants. Sociologist Will Herberg, in his 1955 work *Protestant, Catholic, Jew*, noted the irony of the Protestant alliance with the author of *American Freedom and Catholic Power*. A growing Protestant "minority-group defensiveness," he explained, "has contributed greatly toward turning an important segment of American Protestantism into a vehement champion of an extreme doctrine of the separation of church and state." He further explained, "Minority-group defensiveness and fear of 'Rome' have tended to drive American Protestantism into a strange alliance with the militant secularist anti-Catholicism that is associated with the recent work of Paul Blanshard."[9]

Conservative Protestant respect for Blanshard as an authority on Catholicism could even be seen in the new publication *Christianity Today*, founded by the well-known Evangelical leader, Billy Graham. Articles in *Christianity Today* exhibited a fear of Catholic power and a significant association of resistance to birth control with the Catholic Church. For example, an article in an August 1958 issue told the story of a commissioner of hospitals in New York who forbade a doctor from prescribing birth control to a Protestant woman. The

---

[8]Blanshard, *American Freedom and Catholic Power*, 108–9.

[9]Will Herberg, *Protestant, Catholic, Jew: An Essay in American Religious Sociology*, rev. ed. (Garden City, NY: Anchor Books, 1960), 235.

article did not take a stand on the issue of birth control specifically, but it started out by exclaiming "Danger! Precedent! Such is the cry of Protestants and Other Americans United for the Separation of Church and State which this summer voiced misgivings over such potential pacesetters as these." It went on to quote a POAU spokesman who explained that this was the sort of thing many people feared would be the result of increasing Catholic influence in the political realm.[10]

Despite this portrayal of birth control as a Catholic issue, further articles in *Christianity Today* expressed that some conservative Protestants still had doubts as to its morality. An article in a December 1959 issue brought up Protestant reactions to a statement made by the U.S. Catholic Bishops in which the bishops condemned public assistance for birth control. The article explained that Protestant opinion was divided over birth control, but that many Protestants had been searching for the truth regarding the matter, and that, "prodded by controversy, many went anew to the Bible for a re-examination of views on the legitimacy of sex severed from its procreative role."[11] As a number of other articles in *Christianity Today* showed, these reexaminations placed just as much emphasis on the world population problem as they did on the words of Scripture.[12]

---

[10]"Church and State," *Christianity Today*, August 18, 1958, 27–28.

[11]"Evangelicals Face up to Birth Control Issue," *Christianity Today*, December 21, 1959, 31.

[12]"Evangelicals Face up to Birth Control Issue." For examples, see also E.P. Schulze, "Limitation of Offspring," *Christianity Today*, February 1, 1960, 40–41; Harold B. Kuhn, "Current Religious Thought," *Christianity Today*, July 17, 1964, 40. One editorialist complained about the emphasis placed on the population problem in debates over birth control, saying they "frequently . . . involve earnest churchmen in sheer relativism." He further complained that "attempts to justify birth control by appeal to population explosions come dangerously close to making the end justify the means." See "Exploding Populations and Birth Control," *Christianity Today*, February 1, 1960, 22–23.

In her *Social History of Oral Contraceptives*, Elizabeth Siegel Watkins claims that "by the late 1950s, the large majority of married people, with the exception of Roman Catholics, accepted and used birth control." She states that by this time, "most Americans were not troubled by the moral implications of contraception and the separation of sexual intercourse from procreation."[13] The concern over world population growth that influenced conservative Protestant debate on birth control also played a prominent role in the 1958 Lambeth Conference's removal of any remaining strictures on the use of birth control by married couples. While the 1930 Lambeth Conference had cautiously allowed the use of birth control for serious reasons, Lambeth 1958 expressed unreserved support for and even encouragement of the practice:

> The Conference believes that the responsibility for deciding upon the number and frequency of children has been laid by God upon the consciences of parents everywhere; that this planning, in such ways as are mutually acceptable to husband and wife in Christian conscience ... should be the result of positive choice before God. Such responsible parenthood, built on obedience to all the duties of marriage, requires a wise stewardship of the resources and abilities of the family as well as a thoughtful consideration of the varying population needs and problems of society and the claims of future generations.[14]

The extent to which population concerns factored into the 1958 Lambeth declaration in favor of birth control was obvious. One commentator said that "on this occasion, at least,

---

[13]Elizabeth Siegel Watkins, *On the Pill: A Social History of Oral Contraceptives, 1950–1970* (Baltimore: Johns Hopkins University Press, 1998), 11.

[14]Lambeth Conference 1958, Resolution 115, "The Family in Contemporary Society – Marriage," http://www.lambethconference.org/resolutions/1958/1958–115.cfm (accessed January 15, 2011).

it was a case of bishops quoting more from blue books and less from the Bible."[15] This growing religious preoccupation with population growth found expression in the 1960 book *The Population Explosion and Christian Responsibility* by Richard Fagley, a spokesman for the World Council of Churches. In this work, Fagley argued in favor of the acceptance and promotion of birth control by Christian denominations. He said his book was a call to action for Christians to fulfill their obligation of embracing "responsible parenthood," which he claimed was "a doctrine whose time has come."[16]

The Population Explosion and Christian Responsibility directly connected opposition to birth control with the Catholic Church. Fagley suggested that one reason the United Nations and various government organizations had not addressed the population problem was that they did not want to stir up problems with the Church.[17] He conceded that Roman Catholic organizations had a right to use their political influence, but he argued that Protestants did as well. He lamented that they had neglected to do so and complained that their reticence had been a major factor in the inaction of government aid programs. He urged them to reflect on this failure and to resolve to give "a more adequate Christian witness" in order that governments might come to take a "more realistic approach" to the problem of increasing world population. In Fagley's view, the use of birth control was not merely a choice to be made by Christian couples, but a moral necessity to be sponsored by government agencies. Fortunately, he said, Christians were becoming more attuned to this thinking. "Day

---

[15]Flan Campbell, "Birth Control and the Christian Churches," in Garrett Hardin, ed., *Population, Evolution and Birth Control: A Collage of Controversial Ideas*, 2nd ed. (San Francisco: W.H. Freeman, 1969), 218. "Blue books" referred to statistical reports of population growth.

[16]Richard M. Fagley, *The Population Explosion and Christian Responsibility* (New York: Oxford University Press, 1960), 4–5.

[17]Fagley, *The Population Explosion*, 8, 94.

by day," he explained, "the fears and inhibitions of the past pass away."[18]

While Protestant fears of birth control may have been passing away, fear of Catholic power in the United States continued. In 1960, Americans once again faced the prospect of a Catholic president. As with the 1928 political aspirations of Al Smith, the campaign of John F. Kennedy once more raised the specter of a United States government under the control of Rome.[19] The association of opposition to birth control with the Catholic Church played a prominent role in the election. Sanger herself worried about what a Kennedy victory would mean for her movement. Paul Blanshard recounted that she "announced that if Kennedy be elected President she would leave the country."[20] Indeed, the Catholic teaching against birth control shadowed Kennedy all along the campaign trail, and he frequently found himself explaining that the religious teachings of his Church would not influence his executive deci-

---

[18]Fagley, *The Population Explosion*, 9–10. Conservative Christians did debate the relevance of Fagley's book. Many heeded his call, but not all. In a review of the book for *Christianity Today*, Sherwood W. Wirt questioned Fagley's proposed solution, saying, "The truth is, God has always confounded the statisticians. One has a feeling that by the year A.D. 2000 such books as this will be seen to have been looking in the wrong places." The publication of Fagley's book was a significant point in the last stages of the Protestant debate over birth control, but in 1960, his book was overshadowed by an even more important event in the history of the birth control movement. That event was the release of the oral contraceptive commonly known as "the pill" by Dr. Gregory Pincus and co-inventor Dr. John Rock. While Pincus was Jewish, birth control historian Andrea Tone describes Rock as a "devout Catholic." He was "the father of five and grandfather of fourteen, he attended Mass daily and kept a crucifix on the wall above his office desk." She says he was also conservative on many social issues, but was openly progressive on birth control, having instructed students in birth control methods while a professor at Harvard Medical School and also having sided against the Church during the referendum in Massachusetts. See Andrea Tone, *Devices and Desires: A History of Contraceptives in America* (New York: Hill and Wang, 2001), 216. After Paul VI's condemnation of birth control in 1968, Rock became disillusioned with the church.

sions regarding such matters. While addressing the American Society of Newspaper editors, he found himself questioned yet again as to whether he would allow his religious affiliation to interfere with any possible federal legislation on birth control. Shaun Casey, a recent chronicler of the campaign, explains that Kennedy "was frustrated that although he had given clear answer to this, that did not prevent the charge being made against him."[21]

Kennedy's reassurances that he would not allow himself to be influenced by the Catholic hierarchy eventually put the fears of many non-Catholic Americans to rest and helped him become the nation's first Catholic president. At the same time, the campaign questions put to him regarding birth control showed the extent to which non-Catholic Americans still worried that the Catholic Church would attempt to force its moral prohibitions against birth control on them. While these fears now seem unrealistic in light of Kennedy's largely secular presidency, the fact that the heavily Catholic-populated states of Massachusetts and Connecticut technically still had anti-birth-control laws in 1960 made non-Catholic concern seem

---

[19]Philip Jenkins describes the extreme anti-Catholicism exhibited during the campaign, saying that "during the 1960 presidential election, even the most ancient and discredited pornographic fantasies were again pressed into service." He explains, "Democrats had to confront such scabrous titles as *Abolish the Nunneries and Save the Girls*, *Convent Life Unveiled*, *The Convent Horror*, *I Married a Monk*, and those ludicrous old warhorses, *Maria Monk* and *The Priest, the Woman and the Confessional*. Other tracts depicted priestly inquisitors torturing heroic Protestant dissidents." See Philip Jenkins, *The New Anti-Catholicism: The Last Acceptable Prejudice* (Oxford: Oxford University Press), 45.

[20]Paul Blanshard, *Personal and Controversial*, 35. Additionally, Blanshard explained, "In her early years Margaret Sanger was far more anti-Catholic than I was."

[21]Shaun A. Casey, *The Making of a Catholic President: Kennedy vs. Nixon, 1960* (New York: Oxford University Press, 2009.), 72.

more reasonable.[22] It took a U.S. Supreme Court decision to finally remove these laws.

In 1965, Sanger's birth control movement won a major victory when the Supreme Court in *Griswold v. Connecticut* struck down remaining state anti-birth-control laws.[23] Writing the majority opinion, Justice William Douglas presented a view of the nature of marriage that differed significantly from that which Pius XI described in 1930. He explained that "marriage is a coming together for better or for worse, hopefully enduring, and intimate to the degree of being sacred. It is an association that promotes a way of life, not causes; a harmony in living, not political faiths; a bilateral loyalty, not commercial or social projects."[24] Despite his declaration that marriage did not promote "social causes," Douglas's description of it as "hopefully enduring" fell more in line with Sanger's new, pragmatic morality than with the absolute moral view presented in *Casti Connubii*. Sanger, her life's work now complete with the court's ruling against the remaining Comstock laws, died the following year.

Chroniclers of the birth control movement like to point out the appropriateness of the timing of Sanger's death. At eighty-six years old, she had come a long way from her early days of publishing the *Woman Rebel*. Legal prohibitions against birth control were all but gone, most religious denominations accepted birth control as morally licit, and the sexual revolution of the 1960s seemed a good indication that the new civilization she hoped for had come to fruition.[25] One event she

---

[22]These laws were mostly left-over state Comstock laws from the preceding century.

[23] The Connecticut law struck down by the Court was hardly ever enforced.

[24]Griswold v. Connecticut, 381 U.S. 479 (1965).

[25]It was not until the 1972 case of *Eisenstadt v. Baird* that the Supreme Court extended the right to birth control to unmarried couples.

surely desired but did not get to see was the allowance of birth control use by her "arch-enemy," the Catholic Church. If she had lived a few more years and seen the result of the Church's discussion on the matter, she would have been sorely disappointed.

In the 1960s, many people hoped the Catholic Church would modernize its moral teaching and lift its prohibition on birth control. Indeed, a number of prominent Catholic doctors and intellectuals such as John Rock and John Noonan recommended that very thing.[26] Pope John XXIII fueled these hopes by opening the Second Vatican Council in October 1962. The council quickly became involved with the task of *aggiornamento*, or bringing the Church up to date with the modern world. Many progressives thought this would include an updating of the Church's teaching on birth control, but the newly elected Pope Paul VI decided to reserve the addressing of this matter to himself. He enlarged the commission his predecessor had created to study the issue, and in 1966 that commission concluded its work with a report in which the majority of its members endorsed a change in the official Catholic stance on birth control. The world held its breath, waiting for the Church to update its teaching and get in step with modern society.

When a papal pronouncement finally came in 1968, it came in the form of Paul VI's encyclical letter *Humanae Vitae*, which reaffirmed the Catholic Church's endorsement of marital procreation and its condemnation of artificial means of birth control. The pope began the encyclical by acknowledging that many changes had taken place in society which made it necessary to reexamine the Church's teaching on the matter, but like Pius XI before him, he expressed the duty of the Church to uphold the natural moral law laid down by God. In

---

[26]See John Rock, *The Time Has Come: A Catholic Doctor's Proposals to End the Battle Over Birth Control* (New York: Knopf, 1963); and, John Noonan, *Contraception: A History of Its Treatment by the Catholic Theologians and Canonists* (Cambridge: Belknap Press of Harvard University Press, 1965).

the letter, he first condemned abortion and then went on to declare:

> Equally to be excluded, as the teaching authority of the Church has frequently declared, is direct sterilization, whether perpetual or temporary, whether of the man or of the woman. Similarly excluded is every action which, either in anticipation of the conjugal act, or in its accomplishment, or in the development of its natural consequences, proposes, whether as an end or as a means, to render procreation impossible.[27]

Most of the world, including many Catholics, did not respond well to *Humanae Vitae*. Many of the Catholic laity and even numerous priests openly voiced their opposition. Some priests went so far as to sign a public denunciation of the encyclical in the *New York Times*. Countless lay Catholic couples chose to simply ignore the Church's ban.[28] Among Protestant leaders, Eugene Carlson Blake, general secretary of the World Council of Churches, complained that *Humanae Vitae* put the Catholic Church back where it had started in its discussions on birth control and that "the Roman Catholic position as now stated depends too much upon an old conception of natural law to be persuasive to twentieth-century man." Likewise, Billy Graham said of *Humanae Vitae*, "In general, I would disagree with it ... I believe in planned parenthood." The Archbishop of Canterbury, Arthur Michael Ramsey,

---

[27]Paul VI, *Humanae Vitae*, 1968, in Papal Encyclicals Online, http://www.papalencyclicals.net/Paul06/p6humana.htm (accessed December 3, 2010).

[28]Gene Burns, *The Frontiers of Catholicism: The Politics of Ideology in a Liberal World* (Berkeley, CA: University of California Press, 1992), 68, 101. Mass public dissent on a moral issue of this kind would have been extremely unusual among American Catholics before the Second Vatican Council. In the 1960s, however, changes at the council and in society broke down the unity and monolithic image of the Church. See Patrick Allitt, *Catholic Intellectuals and Conservative Politics in America: 1950–1985* (Ithaca, NY: Cornell University Press, 1993), 5.

agreed with Blake and Graham and stated that the moral teachings contained in *Humanae Vitae* were not in agreement with those of the Anglican Church since the 1958 Lambeth Conference. He said that, judging from the population problems the world was facing, the conclusions of the Lambeth Conference were more appropriate.[29]

Commentaries on *Humane Vitae* by such Protestant leaders as Blake and Ramsey showed the extent to which they had embraced Sanger's new morality. They decried Pope Paul VI's reliance on a fixed natural law and argued that moral teaching on birth control needed to be updated in light of the world's population problem. Despite his own committee's recommendation to the contrary, the pope resisted popular pressure for a change in moral teaching and reasserted the Catholic condemnation of birth control based upon fixed natural law. Had Sanger still been alive, she undoubtedly would have had some comments of her own about the pope's decision, despite the fact that *Griswold* had largely eliminated her need for birth control propaganda, at least in the United States. Amid much strong criticism, *Humanae Vitae*, like *Casti Connubii* almost four decades before it, set down a clear line on the matter of birth control, and placed the Catholic Church firmly in the anti-birth-control camp. While many Catholic scholars tried to reason around it, most people realized the significance of the pope's action. With the promulgation of the encyclical, opposition to birth control—more concretely than ever before—became a defining mark of the Catholic Church.

---

[29]"Pope Faces Birth Control Crisis," *Christianity Today*, August 16, 1968, 42 (Ellipsis original).

CONCLUSION

Pope Paul VI's promulgation of *Humane Vitae* in 1968 once again sharply drew the battle lines in the fight over birth control, and the opposing forces gradually settled into their trenches. The Catholic Church found itself much more alone in this fight than it had been only a few decades earlier. Most Americans now saw opposition to birth control as a defining characteristic of Catholic moral teaching. As Sanger lay dying in 1966, she could look back over the last half-century, satisfied that she had largely accomplished her goals. The new morality, based on human experience and situational expediency, largely dominated discussions of birth control in non-Catholic circles. The use of birth control was now legal throughout the United States, and most religious bodies had come to accept it as morally permissible. Furthermore, the connection Sanger had sought to draw between opposition to birth control and the Catholic Church had become a reality. Popular opinion embraced and carried on her arguments regarding the scientific backwardness and lust for power of the Church in its continued, unthinking refusal to accept the reality of birth control.

The results of Sanger's campaign have carried into the present day, as shown in the introduction to this work. Though many people interpreted Pope Benedict XVI's 2010 comments regarding condom use as a softening of the Church's stance, he himself clarified that this was not the case, noting in the same interview that the Church did not regard birth control as "a real or moral solution." In further clarifications of Benedict's comments, the Vatican echoed various statements made by Catholic churchmen over the preceding century as it reaffirmed the unchanging nature of morality, explaining that "an action which is objectively evil, even if a lesser evil, can never be licitly willed."[1] Such statements were evidence that the contrast between the Church's traditional moral views and the new morality espoused by Sanger would continue to shape the birth control debate in the foreseeable future.

This book has demonstrated that Margaret Sanger saw her birth control crusade as a revolution against the absolute moral structure represented by the Catholic Church. In order to carry out this revolution, she waged a propaganda campaign against the Church in which she portrayed it as the sole enemy of birth control and, by extension, as the enemy of liberty and science. She did not adopt this course only as a matter of expediency, but was genuinely anti-Catholic at heart and sincerely saw the Church as her enemy. By linking her birth control revolution with the tradition of the American Revolution through the use of patriotic and anti-Catholic rhetoric, she depicted her fight for birth control as a struggle for American freedom against the tyranny of the Catholic Church.

As the years passed, Sanger saw her efforts bear fruit in a number of triumphs for birth control. The majority of religious bodies reversed their moral prohibitions against the practice, and a series of court victories led to the legalization of birth control throughout the United States by 1965. Throughout this same time, the Catholic Church reiterated its condemnation of birth control, allowing Sanger to further her portrayal of the Church as scientifically backward and hostile to liberty. With Paul VI's reaffirmation of the Church's ban in 1968, hopes that the Catholic Church would change its moral teaching subsided, and the popular image of the Church as an

---

[1]Francis X. Rocca, "Vatican Walks Back Any Change to Teaching on Condoms," *Huff Post: Religion*, December 21, 2010. http://www.huffingtonpost.com/2010/12/21/vatican-says-no-change-to_n_799880.html. (accessed June 23, 2014).

outdated institution opposed to birth control, science, and liberty became almost as absolute as its unchanging moral code.

BIBLIOGRAPHY

PRIMARY SOURCES

"Archbishop Hayes on Birth Control." *New York Times*, December 18, 1921. http://proquest.umi.com. Accessed March 7, 2011.

Bell, Ralcy Husted. "In the Name of the Babe of Bethlehem." *Birth Control Review* 6, no. 2 (February 1922): 16–17. In *Birth Control Review*. New York: Da Capo Press, 1970.

Blanshard, Paul. *American Freedom and Catholic Power*. Boston: Beacon Press, 1949.

———. *Personal and Controversial: An Autobiography by Paul Blanshard*. Boston: Beacon Press, 1973.

Campbell, Flan. "Birth Control and the Christian Churches," in Garrett Hardin, ed. *Population, Evolution and Birth Control: A Collage of Controversial Ideas*. 2nd ed. San Francisco: W.H. Freeman, 1969.

"Church and State." *Christianity Today*, August 18, 1958, 27.

Esther Katz, ed., *The Selected Papers of Margaret Sanger, Volume 2: Birth Control Comes of Age, 1928–1939*. Chicago: University of Illinois Press, 2006.

"Evangelicals Face up to Birth Control Issue." *Christianity Today*, December 21, 1959, 31.

"Exploding Populations and Birth Control." *Christianity Today*, February 1, 1960, 22–23.

Fagley, Richard M. *The Population Explosion and Christian Responsibility*. New York: Oxford University Press, 1960.

Herberg, Will. *Protestant, Catholic, Jew: An Essay in American Religious Sociology.* Rev. ed. Garden City, NY: Anchor Books, 1960.

Kuhn, Harold B. "Current Religious Thought." *Christianity Today,* July 17, 1964, 40.

Lambeth Conference 1920. Resolution 68, "Problems of Marriage and Sexual Morality. http://www.lambethconference.org. Accessed March 8, 2011.

Lambeth Conference 1930. Resolution 15, "The Life and Witness of the Christian Community – Marriage and Sex." http://www.lambethconference.org. Accessed March 7, 2011.

Lambeth Conference 1958. Resolution 115, "The Family in Contemporary Society – Marriage." http://www.lambethconference.org. Accessed January 15, 2011.

Leo XIII. *Diuturnum.* June 29, 1881. Vatican: The Holy See. http://www.vatican.va. Accessed January 17, 2011.

———. *Humanum Genus.* April 20, 1884. Vatican: The Holy See. http://www.vatican.va. Accessed January 17, 2011.

———. *Quod Apostolici Muneris.* December 28, 1878, in Papal Encyclicals Online. http://www.papalencyclicals.net. Accessed January 17, 2011.

Noonan, John. *Contraception: A History of Its Treatment by the Catholic Theologians and Canonists.* Cambridge: Belknap Press of Harvard University Press, 1965.

Paul VI. *Humanae Vitae.* 1968. In Papal Encyclicals Online. http://www.papalencyclicals.net. Accessed December 3, 2010.

Pius IX. *Nostis et Nobiscum.* December 8, 1849. In Papal Encyclicals Online. http://www.papalencyclicals.net. Accessed January 17, 2011.

Pius XI. *Casti Connubii,* December 1930. Vatican: The Holy See. inhttp://www.vatican.va. Accessed January 17, 2011.

"Pope Faces Birth Control Crisis." *Christianity Today,* August 16, 1968, 42.

Rock, John. *The Time Has Come: A Catholic Doctor's Proposals to End the Battle Over Birth Control.* New York: Knopf, 1963.

Sanger, Margaret. "At Long Last." *New Masses* (July 6, 1937): 19–20. In The Public Writings and Speeches of Margaret Sanger. http://www.nyu.edu/projects/sanger/webedition/app/documents/show.php?sangerDoc=224215.xml. Accessed December 16, 2013. (Hereafter cited as PWS).

————. "Birth Control Advances: A Reply to the Pope." 1931. http://www.nyu.edu/projects/sanger/webedition. Accessed December 14, 2010.

————. "Birth Control." *The Melting Pot* (July 1916): 5–6. In PWS. Accessed December 14, 2010.

————. "*Catholics and Birth Control.*" *New Republic* 79, no. 1019 (June 13, 1934): 129, In PWS. Accessed December 14, 2010.

————. "Church Control?" *Birth Control Review* 5 no. 12 (December 1921): 3–4. In *Birth Control Review.* New York: Da Capo Press, 1970.

————. "Fabian Hall Speech." Draft. July 5, 1915. In PWS. Accessed December 14, 2010.

————. "Facing the New Year." *Birth Control Review* (January 1923): 3–4. In PWS. Accessed December 14, 2010.

————. *Margaret Sanger, An Autobiography.* 1838. Reprint, New York: Dover Publications, 1971.

————. "Modern Schools in Spain." *The Modern School* (May 1916): 5–9. In PWS. Accessed December 14, 2010.

————. *My Fight for Birth Control.* New York: Farrar and Rinehart, 1931.

————. "One Week's Activity in England," *Birth Control Review* (August 1925): 219–20. In PWS. Accessed December 14, 2010.

————. "Our Fight in New York." *Birth Control Review* (December 1922): 241. In PWS. Accessed December 14, 2010.

————. "Reply by Margaret Sanger to Archbishop Hayes' Statement." (January 20 1922). In PWS. Accessed December 14, 2010.

————. "The Civilizing Force of Birth Control." 1929. In Calverton and S.D. Schmalhausen, eds. *Sex in Civilization* (Garden City, NY, 1939), 525–37. In PWS. Accessed December 14, 2010.

————. "The Morality of Birth Control." Published Speech. New York, 1921. In PWS. Accessed December 14, 2010.

Schulze, E.P. "Limitation of Offspring," *Christianity Today*, February 1, 1960, 40–41.

The Mike Wallace Interview. September 21, 1957. Harry Ransom Center: The University of Texas at Austin website. http://www.hrc.utexas.edu/multimedia/video/2008/wallace/sanger_margaret.html. Accessed March 17, 2011.

"The Press Protests," *Birth Control Review* 5 no. 12 (December 1921): 16–17. In *Birth Control Review.* New York: Da Capo Press, 1970.

SECONDAY SOURCES

Allitt, Patrick. *Catholic Intellectuals and Conservative Politics in America: 1950–1985*. Ithaca, NY: Cornell University Press, 1993.

Burns, Gene. *The Frontiers of Catholicism: The Politics of Ideology in a Liberal World*. Berkeley, CA: University of California Press, 1992.

———. *The Moral Veto: Framing Contraception, Abortion, and Cultural Pluralism in the United States*. New York: Cambridge University Press, 2005.

Carey, Patrick W. *Catholics in America: A History*. Westport, CT: Praeger, 2004.

Carlson, Allan. *Godly Seed: American Evangelicals Confront Birth Control, 1873–1973*. New Brunswick, NJ: Transaction Publishers, 2012.

Casey, Shaun A. *The Making of a Catholic President: Kennedy vs. Nixon, 1960*. New York: Oxford University Press, 2009.

Chesler, Ellen. *Woman of Valor: Margaret Sanger and the Birth Control Movement in America*. New York, Simon & Schuster, 1992.

Davies, Sharon. *Rising Road: A True Tale of Love, Race, and Religion in America*. Oxford: Oxford University Press, 2010.

Dolan, Jay P. *In Search of an American Catholicism: A History of Religion and Culture in Tension*. New York: Oxford University Press, 2002.

Dolan, Jay P. *The American Catholic Experience: A History from Colonial Times to the Present*. Garden City, NY: Image Books of Doubleday, 1987.

Douglas, Emily Taft. *Margaret Sanger: Pioneer of the Future*. New York: Holt, Rinehart and Winston, 1970.

Ellis, John Tracy. *American Catholicism*. Chicago: The University of Chicago Press, 1956.

Esther Katz, ed., *The Selected Papers of Margaret Sanger, Volume 2: Birth Control Comes of Age, 1928–1939*. Chicago: University of Illinois Press, 2006.

———. "The Editor as Public Authority: Interpreting Margaret Sanger." *The Public Historian* 17, no. 1 (Winter 1995): 41–50.

Flynn, George Q. *American Catholics and the Roosevelt Presidency: 1932–36.* Lexington: University of Kentucky Press, 1968.

Fogarty, Gerald P. "North America." In Adrian Hastings, ed., *Modern Catholicism: Vatican II and After.* New York: Oxford University Press, 1991.

Franchot, Jenny. *Roads to Rome: The Antebellum Protestant Encounter with Catholicism.* Berkeley, CA: University of California Press, 1994.

Hall, Ruth. *Passionate Crusader: The Life of Marie Stopes.* New York: Harcourt Brace Jovanovich, 1977.

Hennesey, James. *American Catholics: A History of the Roman Catholic Community in the United States,* paperback ed. New York: Oxford University Press, 1983.

Higham, John. *Strangers in the Land: Patterns in American Nativism.* New York: Atheneum, 1963.

Jenkins, Philip. *The New Anti-Catholicism: The Last Acceptable Prejudice.* Oxford: Oxford University Press, 2003.

Kennedy, David M. *Birth Control in America: The Career of Margaret Sanger.* New Haven: Yale University Press, 1970.

Lader, Lawrence. *The Margaret Sanger Story and the Fight for Birth Control.* Garden City, NY: Doubleday & Company, 1955.

Lichtman, Allan J. *Prejudice and the Old Politics: The Presidential Election of 1928.* Chapel Hill, NC: University of North Carolina Press, 1979.

McAvoy, Thomas T. *A History of the Catholic Church in the United States.* Notre Dame, IN: University of Notre Dame Press, 1969.

McGreevy, John T. *Catholicism and American Freedom: A History.* New York: W.W. Norton, 2003.

McLaren, Angus. *A History of Contraception: From Antiquity to the Present Day.* Oxford: Basil Blackwell, 1990.

Moore, Edmund A. *A Catholic Runs for President: The Campaign of 1928.* New York: The Ronald Press Company, 1956.

Nordstrom, Justin. *Danger on the Doorstep: Anti-Catholicism and American Print Culture in the Progressive Era.* Notre Dame, IN: University of Notre Dame Press, 2006.

Rose, June. *Marie Stopes and the Sexual Revolution.* London: Faber and Faber, 1992.

Sanger, Alexander. *Beyond Choice: Reproductive Freedom in the 21st Century.* New York: PublicAffairs, 2004.

Tentler, Leslie. "The Abominable Crime of Onan": Catholic Pastoral Practice and Family Limitation in the United States, 1875–1919." *Church History* 71, no. 2 (June 2002): 307–340.

Tentler, Leslie. *Catholics and Contraception: An American History.* Ithaca, NY: Cornell University Press, 2004.

Tobin, Kathleen. *The American Religious Debate Over Birth Control, 1907–1937.* Jefferson, NC: McFarland & Company, 2001.

Tobin-Schlesinger, Kathleen. "Population and Power: The Religious Debate over Contraception, 1916–1936." PhD diss., University of Chicago, 1994. In ProQuest Dissertations and Theses, http://proquest.umi.com. Accessed February 2, 2011.

Tone, Andrea. *Devices and Desires: A History of Contraceptives in America.* New York: Hill and Wang, 2001.

Watkins, Elizabeth Siegel. *On the Pill: A Social History of Oral Contraceptives, 1950–1970.* Baltimore: Johns Hopkins University Press, 1998.

Index

About the Author

Nicholas Kaminsky earned a B.A. in History from Bethany Lutheran College, Mankato, Minnesota in 2008 and an M.A. in History from Minnesota State University, Mankato in 2011. While in graduate school, he focused on the area of religion in the United States. He has taught a broad range of history courses, from ancient world civilizations to modern America, at Bethany Lutheran College, with additional teaching experience at Blessed José Sánchez del Río Minor Seminary, Mankato. He has also presented research in several scholarly venues and has worked on a U.S. congressional campaign. When he is not busy poring over old books or microfilm, he enjoys the outdoors, good food, and time spent with family and friends.

CPSIA information can be obtained at www.ICGtesting.com
Printed in the USA
LVOW04s0745021015

456655LV00017B/197/P

9 780985 754334